All American Yemeni Girls

All American Yemeni Girls

Being Muslim in a Public School

LOUKIA K. SARROUB

PENN

University of Pennsylvania Press

Philadelphia

10 9 8 7 6 5 4 3 2 1

Published by
University of Pennsylvania Press
Philadelphia, Pennsylvania 19104-4011

Library of Congress Cataloging-in-Publication Data

Sarroub, Loukia K.
    All American Yemeni girls : being Muslim in a public school / Loukia K. Sarroub.
      p.   cm.
    Includes bibliographical references and index.
    ISBN 0-8122-3833-8 (cloth : alk. paper) — ISBN 0-8122-1894-9 (pbk. : alk. paper)
    1. Yemenite Americans—Michigan—Dearborn—Social conditions.   2. Yemenite
Americans—Michigan—Dearborn—Ethnic identity.   3. Yemenite Americans—
Education—Michigan—Dearborn.   4. Muslims—Michigan—Dearborn—Social
conditions.   5. Teenage girls—Michigan—Dearborn—Social conditions.   6. High
school students—Michigan—Dearborn—Social conditions.   7. Dearborn (Mich.)—
Ethnic relations.   8. Public schools—Social aspects—Michigan—Dearborn.
9. Education—Social aspects—Michigan—Dearborn.   10. United States—Ethnic
relations—Case studies.   I. Title.

F574.D2S37   2005
305.235'2'08992753307433—dc22

                                                                        2004052027

For my parents,
Abdelkader Sarroub and Georgia Janavara Sarroub

Contents

Chapter 1

Introduction: Being American, Being Yemeni

Uncovering a Predicament

Okay, in their eyes, it means you be quiet, you listen, you obey and you go through, you listen to what we say, regardless, because we know what's best for you. Okay, in my eyes, it's not. It's you take what they say into consideration but you also see your own views. You try to—you have to make the decision on your own. You have to go beyond just what they say, what they're demanding and look at it and look at what you want, how do you see it, how do you feel about it, what is the best outcome for you. Because you know yourself best. . . . For me, see, I consider everything in an Islamic point of view. And being Yemeni, that's basically, you listen to what they say. Being Americanized is the fact that you can stand up and say, "No," you know, "This is what I want. And this is the reason why I want this."

In 1998, Saba's hands and fingers punctuated each thought as she spoke with the slight staccato that is characteristic of English speech influenced by Arabic.[1] Except for her face and hands, Saba's body was completely covered as she sat across from me, explaining how difficult it is to construct an identity that makes sense in the American and Yemeni Muslim worlds she inhabits. This was not the first of our conversations on this topic, but it was the most emotional. Saba was tired, emotionally stressed to a breaking point, and depressed. Yet she shared her thoughts with me freely as the audio recorder blinked after each pause, recording not only her words but also the strain of her efforts to make sense of her life. As I listened and responded to her comments, I thought of the other Yemeni American girls with whom I had talked. Their families settled in the United States in the early 1970s, and all of them felt the same optimism and desperation Saba expressed; all of them were attempting to reconcile the American lives they experienced at school with the Yemeni lives they knew at home; all of them wanted to succeed at being good students and good daughters and wives; and all of them felt as if they were failing at being both American and Yemeni. They each feared the risk of becoming less than "good Muslim women."

In my attempt to understand the lives of these girls and their peers, I find that meaning is both uncovered and re-covered. At times this is as simple as wearing or removing the *hijab* (scarf) from one's head. In other instances, the actions, the words, the cast of one's eyes—these index the undercurrents of meaning. Telling this story means being able to navigate among meanings, and therefore it is no coincidence that I chose to write ethnography. To understand the Yemeni American girls in the context of a "Yemeni village" in the United States, it is important to focus on the quotidian as well as the unusual occurrences in that community. Comprehending as much as possible the lives of the Yemeni within the contexts of school, home, and community means applying a broad methodological approach that relies on *thick* description (Geertz 1973) based on rigorous observation and participant and nonparticipant observations, including "shadowing," formal interviews, and informal conversations. This ethnography is based on twenty-six months of fieldwork in a Yemeni community in the Southend of Dearborn, Michigan, from 1997 to 1999. Local people call it the "Southend" to denote its separate identity, and henceforth I use that label. I returned to Dearborn, in the winter of 2002, to conduct interviews with some of the girls following the September 11, 2001, attacks on the New York City World Trade Center towers and the Pentagon. These interviews also took place after I had viewed a CBS *60 Minutes* segment on Dearborn that featured people with whom I had worked.

By describing both the unusual and the mundane and by synthesizing emerging patterns across contexts and the published literature, especially relevant studies conducted on Islam and immigration in Europe, I attempt to contribute to our knowledge about the intersections of education and religion, home and school worlds, and immigrant students and their teachers. U.S. scholars in education tend not to focus, for the most part, on issues such as religion and its impact on education, schooling, home, and community life.[2]

Margery Wolf (1992) has said, "an anthropologist listens to as many voices as she can and then chooses among them when she passes their opinions on to members of another culture. The choice is not arbitrary, but then neither is the testimony" (11). In many ways there is really nothing arbitrary about the site or the participants in this study. They are not representative of all schools or teachers or students or communities across the United States. They were chosen because they are unique. At the same time, however, they belong to larger communities that are not at all unique in that their geopolitical relations are similar to those of others. The children go to public school as other children do. Their teachers deal with cultural and linguistic differences as do teachers in different settings. Their parents worry about their children as do other parents. Without exhausting the list of congruencies and similarities, it is important to note that, like many other ethnographies, the value of this study will be in its ability to develop further constructive ideas and theories about larger issues and problems with which educators and researchers grapple. This is accomplished by paying attention to the particulars, and the point is to get to the "heart of the matter," if possible (Geertz 1983; Wolcott 1994).

In writing this ethnography I hope to broaden our understanding of immigrant families in the United States. As the twenty-first century unfolds, we must not forget that a new generation of Americans is in the making. It is often easy to overlook that American children of immigrants often straddle two or more worlds and must negotiate various systems of belief that may not complement one another. That this process is further complicated by a combination of factors such as religion, ethnic identity, gender, language, social economic standing, and school socialization norms emphasizes how much we need to know to make decisions for improving schools and relations among schools, communities, and homes. This book deals with the importance of uncovering the predicament of being an "either/or" and becoming American in the public schools.

Throughout the book, I focus on the notion of success—what it means for Yemeni American girls to successfully negotiate home and school worlds—in order to delineate the various players' (teachers, parents, students) expectations for success in the worlds of home and school. In U.S. public schools, academic performance and social adjustment have been important defining factors of school success. Normative definitions of success such as academic achievement, learning, and GPA have all in one way or another guided students, teachers, and parents in formulating what is expected of students during any given school day in any given year. However, the idea of success becomes more complex when it is woven into a fabric created out of the threads of cultural, religious, linguistic, geographical, national, and even personal forces. For instance, with regard to immigrants, Gibson suggests that "theories of success and attitudes about the value of formal education have their roots in well-defined cultural processes predating migration" (Gibson and Bhachu 1991:64). In other words, folk and personal theories of success are as important in the construction of individual and communal identities within traditional boundaries as they might be in promoting socioeconomic mobility, a broader and more general goal shared by many people regardless of ethnicity, gender, religion, culture, or color. Examining and defining the intersection of home and school expectations for success is one way of categorically establishing the relationships that govern dispositions, language use, social adjustment, and self-actualization among the Yemeni American high school girls.

Culture is intimately tied to conceptions of successfully negotiating home and school worlds. Culture is also a lens for lending significance to human experience because it refers broadly to the ways in which people make sense of their lives. Di Leonardo (1984) and Florio-Ruane (2001) have noted five prevailing notions of culture in the social sciences: 1) cultures are unique and in conflict with one another, 2) culture is passed on intact from generation to generation, 3) immigrants and their offspring have a common static cultural stock usually referred to as ethnicity, 4) the value of cultural knowledge and practices is measured by economic success, and 5) culture is labeled as inadequate or deficient when ethnic groups fail to thrive economically. Florio-Ruane suggests that these rather static conceptions of culture have been the basis of much educational research on immigrant and minority population and should be reexamined. Although these prevailing conceptions of culture are misleading (if not incorrect), they do inadvertently show that there is very little in them that addresses the roles of individuals and the development of identity in different contexts. In the preface to his book, Rosaldo (1993) points out that "questions of culture seem to touch a nerve because they quite quickly become anguished questions of identity" (xxi). Saba's earlier comments about what it means to be American or Yemeni get at the heart of cultural identity and its politics.

Salient notions of culture have been advanced in various fields and disciplines and have become all the more complex and nuanced. In anthropology, for instance, Ogbu (1988) has defined culture as indexed by artifacts that have symbolic meaning for a population, and the imperatives of culture include people's economic, political, religious, and social institutions, such as schools. In sociology Bourdieu (1977) argues that the process of education and schooling becomes "the production of the habitus, that system of dispositions which acts as a mediation between structures and practice" (487). In other words, culture is both historical action and the present enactment of that history, and the habitus enables the cultural process as Ogbu has defined it. Enactment (and perhaps the intentional or unintentional reproduction) of one's past (traditions, customs, etc.) is mediated by both behavior and discourse, which can be either an adaptation to or an artifact of culture. As will be illustrated within the Yemeni context, past and present are not easily differentiated, because this community continues to live much as they did in Yemen, while the girls continually attempt to successfully adapt to American life at school and Yemeni life at home. Also, the Yemeni American girls show us that classroom life may be surprisingly liberating because the habitus within which gender roles, as they are part of the girls' ethnic identity, matter less than does school talk. In other words, it is because school talk often rules out students' nonschool discourses that problems of identity arise. In this book, it is precisely the educational "culturalectomy" phenomenon that seems to open new possible identities for young women.[3]

More dynamic conceptions of culture embody the development of identity, which is instrumental in understanding how the Yemeni American girls understand themselves at home and at school. Taylor's (1996) phenomenological view directs attention to the self, how the self ascertains how he or she identifies with the world and thus forms an identity. According to Taylor, identity formation is an ongoing and shifting process, dependent on social, historical, and cultural contexts. This view acknowledges that the self is not tightly tied to time or place, and perhaps it is not tied to status and role, which are negotiated and can shift with every situation. Raissiguier (1994), whose research focuses on Algerian and French working-class women in France, has a particularly germane definition of identity: "[It is the] product of an individual or a group of individuals' interpretation and reconstruction of their personal history and particular social location, as mediated through the cultural and discursive context to which they have access" (26). Thus it can be argued that the process of identity formation is one of socialization as one gains access to social institutions such as family or school, but it also means that rules can be suspended and that the notion of self shifts with time and location. Taken literally, the modern dictionary definition of socialization implies a coercive force whereby individuals must often conform to the common needs of a social group. However, in a different light, it can also be argued, as Bernstein (1977) has done, that socialization creates a safe place for people. He understands the process of socialization to mean a child's acquisition of a specific cultural identity that becomes a standard which he or she uses to respond to events, actions, and other individuals: "Socialization sensitizes the child to various orderings of society as these are made substantive in the various roles he is expected to play" (476). What happens when a child is socialized in multiple cultures? Does identity become fragmented according to context (home, school, and community)? And do conceptions of the self also reflect this fragmentation as students remain Yemeni while becoming American?[4] As these questions suggest, success may be somewhat dependent on the *successful* realization of expected selves (or identities) at school, at home, and in the community.

Equally important in the development of identity and its relationship to notions of success is the idea that identity and/or expressions of the self are rooted both in history and in ideology and are often expressed through one's ethnicity. Di Leonardo (1984) defines ethnicity as "a phe-

nomenon of state societies, involving the labeling, from within or without of particular populations as somehow different from the majority"
(23). She argues that the labeling itself, as a cultural process, is crucial
to the construction of identity and ethnicity as groups interact economically and politically. Her work on Italian Americans showed that it matters where Italians came from, when and why they left, where they went,
and how newcomers were received on the basis of economic and social
conditions. Ethnicity, in this view, is both cognitive and economic, and
as the economy changes, so do ethnic boundaries and ideologies. In the
case of the Yemeni as an ethnic group, there is no question that history
and economy affect their worldview with regard to life in the United
States and expectations for success at school and at home. As Gordon
(1964) comments: "Within ethnic groups, persons have two types of
identification that operate simultaneously: historical identification—a
sense of peoplehood shared with other group members—and participation identification—a sense of primary identification with an ethnic
group with whom one shares values and behavioral patterns. Primary
relationships are normally confined to persons who share both these
identifications, persons of the same ethclass, since values and behavior
tend to be related both by class and ethnicity" (89–90). Again, it is clear
that identity formation within a culture is the enactment of both the past
and the present. Identity, then, is dynamic, not static. As di Leonardo
suggests, "Focusing on ethnic boundaries rooted in economic and historical processes allows us instead to see that all of daily life, not just
family life, is part of the construction and reconstruction of ethnic identities" (24). For example, she found that gender identity as well as religious belief changed over generations in the Italian American families
she studied.

The definitional parameters of success—culture, identity, and ethnicity—illustrate the complicated and complex worlds the Yemeni American girls inhabited between home and school. As this ethnography
focuses on girls, gender is also a significant concept and analytic tool
for understanding the high school girls and their community. Gender
identification remains an important aspect of Yemeni and American cultures, and, as such, it must be considered consequential to identity and
ethnic formation. Woods and Hammersley (1993) have suggested that
ethnographers in education must explore the connections between ethnicity and gender rather than rely solely on social class characteristics.
El-Or's (1994) work on ultra-Orthodox Jewish women, for example,
focuses on the intersection of religion and education and the paradox
of educating women in order to foster ignorance and reproduce a static
culture among the women. Finders's (1997) work on the literacy events
of young adolescent girls characterizes the girls' literate world as consti-

tuting both the official school literacy practices and the "literate under-life." Proweller's (1998) work examines the identity formation processes among a group of upper-middle-class adolescent girls in a private, elite academy. In these studies ethnographers delimit the study of identity in unusual ways where gendered practices are strongly influenced by school life, religion, ethnicity, and language. The representation of gender today is problematic, especially if and when gender itself becomes an objectified category of socialization within academic and education discourse (Connel 1987; Thorne 1997). I maintain that gender is a rather fluid category that cannot easily be demarcated or objectified, because it is indexed by talk, interaction, ethnicity, and, in the case of the Yemeni American girls, religion. In many ways, the Yemeni American girls are "triangulators" of identity, and, as a result, culture is enacted in the in-between spaces they occupy in their home and school worlds.[5]

One aim of this book is to argue that the broad concepts described previously must be considered together as factors that help shed light on the continuities and discontinuities that may exist between home and school. During fieldwork in Dearborn, Michigan, I asked the following questions:

- What are the expectations for success at school and at home among Muslim Yemeni American students?
  - How do the girls negotiate the various expectations around them?
- In light of the cultural and/or religious discontinuities that may exist between home and school, how do Yemeni American students make sense of their identities in those contexts?
  - How do the girls develop their identities, between home and school, in a Yemeni and American community?
- What role does gender play in the enactment of cultural norms at home and at school?
- How do ethnicity, religion, and socioeconomic standing influence expectations for success at home and at school?
  - How are these expectations (from parents, teachers, peers) communicated to the girls?
  - And how then do they respond?
- How does the school perceive and accommodate cultural and religious differences among its students?
  - How do teachers view their pedagogical roles with regard to these students?
  - And what impact do school and teacher accommodations have on the students?

I draw mainly from three interdisciplinary perspectives—literacy studies and sociolinguistics, cultural anthropology, and sociology—to explain the relationships and connections among the contexts of school, community, and home. A sociolinguistic perspective is useful in unmasking the notion of culture as discourse (Gee 1989; Goffman 1959, 1981) or ways of being that encompass talk, action, and performance. This frame of reference is especially helpful in delineating the contextual uses of texts and language among the Yemeni American students. For example, the use of Arabic in school serves important functional and religious purposes as students attempt to maintain dual identities. It is not clear, however, whether cultural differences in communication style between home and school have a direct cause-and-effect relationship on school achievement (Erickson 1987). While in the field, I observed that communication style (the discourses used) is important in making social adjustments within the school setting and, in particular, in the classroom, but not necessarily in academic performance. For these students, social success in school (behaving appropriately according to cultural and religious traditions) is as important as academic achievement because the enactment of appropriate social mores in and out of school determines status as well as degrees of shame and honor.

For example, in their study of home and classroom life, Shultz, Florio, and Erickson (1982) observed that there was a mismatch between the teacher's expectations for classroom behavior and her Italian American students' knowledge of the required norms for proper behavior. Shultz and his colleagues found that although the students' social etiquette was perfectly acceptable at home, it did not meet the expectations of the classroom. They concluded that teachers and researchers should attempt to "understand more fully children's socialization into communicative traditions at home and at school, traditions that may be mutually congruent or incongruent" (91). It is clear that those who have studied the impact of home cultures and social class on success at home and in school have concluded that although socioeconomic standing is a useful tool, it does not always explain how individuals learn, produce knowledge, and sustain cultural and/or social identities in multiple worlds. Heath (1983), for instance, showed that the complex language socialization process is "more powerful than single-factor explanations accounting for academic success" (344).

In connection to literacy and sociolinguistic processes, I draw on Ogbu's (1982, 1993) cultural-ecological model, which maintains that child rearing in the family and subsequent adolescent socialization aim at developing instrumental competencies—defined as "the ability to perform a culturally specific task, or a set of functional or instrumental skills"—required for adult economic, political, and social roles. Cultural imperatives vary from one population to another as do the required competencies. Within this model, Ogbu takes issue with views of human development that assume that a child's later school success depends on the acquisition of white middle-class competencies (and sources of cultural capital) through white middle-class child-rearing practices (see Ogbu 1991). He argues that all children experience initial discontinuities between home and school in language use, contextual learning, and style of learning. A central distinction in Ogbu's (1987) account is between voluntary and involuntary minorities. Voluntary minorities are immigrants who "have generally moved to their present societies because they believed that the move would lead to more economic well-being, better overall opportunities or greater political freedom" (317). Involuntary minorities, on the other hand, were brought to the present society through conquest or forced displacement.

Ogbu further differentiates between primary and secondary cultural differences. Primary cultural differences are those that existed before two populations came into contact, whereas secondary ones are those arising after two populations have been in continuous contact and the minority population has participated in the institutions controlled by the majority. Basically Ogbu argues that involuntary minorities face cultural differences based on style, whereas voluntary minorities face differences in content. This means that voluntary minorities or immigrants "perceive their social identity as *primarily different* from the social identity of white Americans" (323), and involuntary minorities "develop a new sense of *social identity in opposition* to the social identity of the dominant group *after they have been subordinated.*" Ogbu argues, "immigrants see the *cultural differences as barriers to overcome* in order to achieve their long-range goals of future employment and *not as markers of identity to be maintained*" (1987:327). Gibson (1988) calls this strategy "accommodation and acculturation without assimilation." In her study of Punjabi Sikh immigrants, she found that although they are proud to be Americans, they "openly and actively reject the notion that Americanization means giving up their separate identity" (24). Involuntary minorities, however, and according to Ogbu's model, perceive cultural differences "they encounter in school as markers of identity to be maintained, not as barriers to be overcome" (331). The cultural-ecological model is useful in assessing what competencies are expected among the Yemeni American girls in the contexts of home, school, and community and how those competencies will influence future success at work and home.

Nevertheless, Ogbu's model has come under criticism in recent years on the grounds that it is not universally applicable. For example, Ogbu omits explaining that primary cultural differences can become charged with political meanings in present situations and actually cause conflict.

In their work, Eldering (1997) and Van Zanten (1997) found that European girls of Arab descent who wore the *hijab* were stigmatized and told to go home by school officials. According to the Associated Press, in a move to emphasize France's secularism, a presidential commission banned Islamic head scarves in public schools on 11 December 2003. As part of a new law, all conspicuous religious symbols, including large Christian crosses and Jewish skullcaps, would be banned in France (Ganley 2003). According to *Le Monde*, the French documented at least 1,256 young French women who wear the scarf in school (Bernard 2003). Debates over the head scarf issue have arisen all over Europe in conjunction with the rise of immigration from predominantly Muslim countries. "The critical factor for the Muslim students seems not to be the origin of the differences—but rather that the differences are viewed as markers of identity" (Gibson 1997). In the case of the Yemeni Americans, they exhibit tendencies that would characterize them as both voluntary and involuntary minorities. Many families are really sojourners who live two lives, one in the United States and a second in Yemen. Furthermore, Ogbu's model does not account for how gender shapes student identity at home and at school and with regard to social and academic performance. In the Yemeni culture, for instance, gender is decidedly a fundamental aspect of social differentiation and must be addressed, especially if school represents a form of liberation as it does for young Muslim girls in Europe and for the Yemeni American girls in Dearborn. In addition, perhaps the most interesting finding in the literature on minority populations is that these students do better in school "when they feel strongly anchored in the identities of their families, communities, and peers and when they feel supported in pursuing a strategy of selective or additive acculturation" (Gibson 1997:445). This is important because it may explain why students who come from working-class families in which the parents (and usually the mother) are semiliterate or print illiterate still perform well, sometimes outperforming the majority population in the school. Finally, Ogbu's model underconceptualizes the power of curriculum and teachers.[6] Schools and teachers have an immense impact on student engagement and achievement in school, and they are often the catalysts needed to change students' futures and future competencies.

From the literature in sociology, I draw on relevant theories relating to social and cultural capital because school performance has often been linked to them. Cultural capital, according to Bourdieu (1987), exists in three forms: the embodied state (dispositions of the mind and body), the objectified state (cultural goods such as books, pictures, instruments, dictionaries, machines, etc.), and the institutionalized state (academic qualifications, which give the holder a conventional, constant, legally guaranteed value with respect to culture). Bourdieu maintains that his theory of cultural reproduction "sought to propose a model of the social mediations and processes which tend, behind the backs of the agents engaged in the school system—teachers, students and their parents—and often against their will, to ensure the transmission of cultural capital across generations and to stamp pre-existing differences in inherited cultural capital with a meritocratic seal of academic consecration by virtue of the special symbolic potency of the [credential]" (Bourdieu and Passeron 1977/1990:ix). In other words and according to this argument, school knowledge and the values transmitted within the institution are more legitimate in society than preexisting home knowledge and values. In accordance with the notion of stamping out preexisting differences, Bourdieu and Passeron (1977/1990) have suggested that "every power which manages to impose meanings and to impose them as legitimate by concealing the power relations which are the basis of its force, adds its own specifically symbolic force to those power relations" (xv).[7] This theory, then, espouses the idea that widely held norms for success, norms that are imposed by schools, are the most meaningful economically and culturally. In contrast to Ogbu's theory of cultural ecology, which accounts for different types of minorities and different types of cultural discontinuities between home and school that are not solely class based, Bourdieu's cultural capital theory instantiates social class as the key factor of success in school. Bourdieu (1977) argues that social class provides individuals who hold high status roles with the resources to maintain positions of power in society. The home and family contribute certain resources, such as language (and forms of discourse) and other types of cultural experiences, which are either in line with or deviate from the middle-class values that schools embody. As Labaree (1997) observes, individuals from low socioeconomic backgrounds aim at upward social mobility by using school as a necessary credential for status positions in society. Yet, according to cultural capital theory, upward mobility and the acquisition of credentials are controlled by one's ability to adopt and enact middle-class values, discourse, and dispositions. In other words, some social class ideologies are better suited to success in schools than others.

In her work on social class and its relationship to parent involvement in schools, Lareau (2000) maintains that the relationship between working-class families and schools is characterized by separation (parents and students think of school and education as a job that stops when the children arrive home). The relationship that middle- to upper-middle-class families have with schools is characterized by interconnectedness, such that the business of school and education is an ongoing endeavor in everyday home life. Meanwhile, schools are thought to accept, reproduce, and reflect societal hierarchies. These ideas were corroborated earlier by Bowles and Gintes (1976), who suggested that schools are class-based institutions that often reproduce the advantages and deficits of class-based consciousness and knowledge. Deterministic in nature, Bowles and Gintes's argument proposed a one-to-one relationship between schools and other societal structures, such as the home. Fortunately this may not really be representative of the levels of congruence and incongruence between home and school environments. In fact, the main thrust of Lareau's argument is that although cultural capital theory improves upon other existing explanations of why middle-class families seem to be more involved in school than working-class families, it needs to be modified if it is to explain that, in fact, "possession of high status cultural resources does not automatically yield a social profit [unless] these cultural resources are activated by the individual" (10). In other words, social class is a potent and at times an accurate predictor of student success in schools, but it may not always account for the enactment of competencies that can cut across social class barriers.

Although cultural reproduction theory provides a strong framework for what schools expect from students in the context of national and/or societal goals, it does not necessarily address the realities of schools and teachers' accommodation of students' differences, whether they be cultural, religious, gender specific, and so on (Cummins 1997; Eisikovits 1997; Eldering 1997; Gibson 1997; Gillborn 1997). If cultural reproduction is viewed mainly as a recursive event, it is challenged by students who have virtually little cultural and/or social capital yet seem to be meeting and exceeding expectations for academic success at school (see Zine 2000 for an analysis of resistance theories and the formation of Islamic subcultures within schools). In the following chapters, I document the religious and cultural traditions that are in fact reproduced and reconstructed within the Yemeni family, and by the girls, and then explore their impact on social and academic performance in the school setting. The evidence will suggest that cultural tools and traditions may have little bearing on learning and achievement but may serve the purpose of easing cultural or religious tensions as home and school worlds collide.

The Hijabat

During my two years in Dearborn, I met, among many others, six high school girls, who became my main research informants, my teachers, and, in the end, my friends. I met these girls at the community center in the Southend, an enclave of Dearborn, and followed them in and out of school and home for two years. They all wore the *hijab* and were therefore called *hijabat* (the plural feminine noun used by these girls and

TABLE 1: THE SIX HIGH SCHOOL *HIJABAT*

Nadya (Grades 9 and 10)	Below average–average
Aisha (Grades 10 and 11)	High achiever
Layla (Grade 10 and 11)	Average
Nouria (Grades 10 and 11)	Average
Saba (Grades 11 and 12)	Above average
Amani (Grades 11 and 12)	Above average

community members to denote those who wear the scarf) by other Arab Americans in the community and in their school. Listed in Table 1 are the girls' names, their grade levels during 1997–99, and their level of achievement in school. High achiever denotes a grade point average of 3.5 or above, above average means a grade point average between 3.0 and 3.5, average denotes a grade point of 3.0, below average denotes a grade point average of 2.0 or below.

Throughout the book, these girls' personalities emerge as highly individualized voices, who, as Brown and Gilligan (1992) suggest in their study of adolescent girls, find themselves at a crossroads of girlhood and womanhood. The *hijabat*'s voices merge and blend into one story about a group of people whose history, ethnicity, religion, school and home lives, and gender delineate social and physical boundaries.

Nadya was a ninth and tenth grader who was characterized by her teachers as having "a lot of potential if only she could settle down." She enjoyed socializing in school, and her school counselor suspected this was so because there were cultural and social constraints in the Yemeni community and at home. Nadya hated to clean and cook at home and knew that her older sister would do her chores. Nadya's parents were careful not to ask her to do too much because she had once had a seizure that frightened her family. So, unlike most of the *hijabat*, Nadya was often excused from her chores, until her older sister was married and moved out of the house.

Aisha was called "very sweet" by all of her friends. She was quiet and rarely spoke. An exceedingly bright student, Aisha dreamed of going to college when I knew her as a tenth and eleventh grader. She tutored at the community center near her home until her parents no longer allowed her to work there. She helped her parents manage their finances and paid the bills. Her biggest worry was whether she would be able to stay in school because her parents wanted to send her to Yemen to marry as her sister had done when she was fifteen. Aisha was afraid to marry one of her cousins because her parents were first cousins, and she worried that there would be phenotypic aberrations, such as missing limbs or blindness. She was concerned all the time with school and her grades and often registered for classes in which she could be with other *hijabat.*

Layla was the most outgoing and talkative of the *hijabat.* She identified strongly with her mother, who grew up among the British when South Yemen was a colony. Layla thought that her mother was more open-minded than most of her friends' mothers. Like many of the *hijabat,* Layla wanted to cut her long hair short and go to college. She kept her personal life and any mention of potential marriage a secret at school and planned to stay single as long as possible, even though there were rumors that she was married. Layla resented learning to cook Yemeni dishes and to maintain a household for her own future home. She had dreams of becoming a teacher, a nurse, or a politician. She tutored at the community center near her home.

Nouria was always dissatisfied with her home and school life. She complained incessantly about her household chores and having to take care of her siblings. More than once, Nouria threatened to commit suicide because she was unhappy. She kept to herself at school when I knew her as a tenth and eleventh grader, but she did tutor at the community center. Most of her energy was spent on finding ways to divorce her husband, also a student in the high school, and trying to persuade her father to let her divorce him. Nouria's older siblings were all high achievers in school, which furthered her disgruntlement. When I returned to Dearborn in 2002, she had run away from home, and her family no longer recognized or acknowledged her as a member of the family.

Saba was known as a leader among the *hijabat.* She could recite the Qur'an in both Arabic and English and gave lectures at the mosque and even organized a weekly lecture and reading group called *Muhathara* (lecture). Saba, as an eleventh and twelfth grader, was a student leader as well and a noted "troublemaker" by the administration and some teachers. Saba tried desperately to obtain permission from her family to choose her own husband and refused to go to Yemen when her family insisted. She tutored and worked in the community health center clinic. She was committed to furthering her education and becoming a teacher or nurse, marrying someone of her choosing, and being a good Muslim.

Amani was quiet and shy. During the tenth and eleventh grades she enrolled in all the preparatory nursing classes and interned at a clinic with her classmates. Amani wanted to become a nurse and planned to attend college. She sometimes wished she could wear short sleeves and take off her scarf but did not think this would be possible in her neighborhood. She drove her brothers to school but was not allowed to work anywhere other than the community center, where she tutored with the other *hijabat.* Amani had to learn how to cook Yemeni dishes at home and was often judged as a worthy cook and housekeeper by relatives and neighbors. She married as soon as she graduated from high school and moved to another state.

The *hijabat*, much like other American women, found themselves hoping to become nurses and teachers—acceptable occupations in their culture. In their community they often said that such occupations preserved their primary roles as mothers and at the same time allowed them to entertain the notion of being educated mothers. For these girls, the prospect of a high school degree, if not a college degree, enhanced the role of the mother in the family. Education is valued by the Yemenis in the United States, and it is especially valued in girls.[8] It is useful to draw a historical contrast between these young women and women at the beginning of the twentieth century in the United States. The shift in women's work roles in the nineteenth century, for example, inspired new definitions of womanhood and eventually led to the feminization of occupations such as teaching. The urbanization and industrialization of the American economy also redefined, to a certain degree, the role women played at home and in society. In tandem with these changes, the advent of universal public education further transformed notions of womanhood, woman's sexuality, and woman's work. I draw attention to this history because Yemeni immigrants also experienced urbanization and industrialization, in their case by means of leaving a mainly agricultural village setting in Yemen for a labor-market-based industry in the United States. The lives of Yemeni women as homemakers today parallel those of many women at the turn of the twentieth century. These transformations, which led to the recognition of teaching as a "woman's profession," are characterized by historians as the "cult of true womanhood" (Clifford 1989; Degler 1980; Ryan 1981), "domestic femininity" (Clifford 1989; Degler 1980; Grumet 1988; Hoffman 1981; Rury 1989); and "domestic/woman's sphere" (Clifford 1989; Ryan 1981). The construction of woman as mother and the paragon of domesticity allowed her to receive an education, but it restrained her in work opportunities. This dialectic of opportunity and constraint illuminates the conflicting private and public roles of women in the last century (Rury 1989). Interestingly enough, I observed that same dialectic among the six *hijabat* and their peers as they attempted to establish their identities at home, in their community, and at school.

A Comment on Methods

Conceptually and methodologicially, the research in this book is based on an interdisciplinary approach. The research conducted during the first year of fieldwork, in 1997–98, was the beginning of a conversation between the published literature and actual field experiences. Prior to being out in the field, notions of ethnicity, identity, culture, gender, and the like seemed relatively clear and uncomplicated. However, negotiating researcher space and identity in the contexts of both the published literature and the field created a dynamic and complex problem. Roland Barthes wrote, "interdisciplinary work, so much discussed these days, is not about confronting already constituted disciplines (none of which, in fact, is willing to let itself go). To do something interdisciplinary it's not enough to choose a 'subject' (a theme) and gather around it two or three sciences. Interdisciplinarity consists in creating a new object that belongs to no one" (quoted in Clifford and Marcus 1986:1). In more ways than one, this project was a new object, not only for me, the researcher, but also for my informants in the schools, homes, and community of Dearborn.

Furthermore, as Kondo (1990) so aptly put it in her research, my own identity was beginning to fragment according to different contexts. One case in point was the uncertainty that the boys in my study would continue to participate during that first year of fieldwork. Only two out of six at the community center agreed to speak with me, and only one allowed me to shadow him once. My very presence as a woman in their school and home lives constituted social embarrassment and peer harassment. The fact is that my work made sense to the Yemeni only in the context of women's lives. As a researcher, this was troublesome to me. One way to deal with this problem was to be less intrusive (not do interviews with the boys) and simply observe, talk, and listen to the boys while shadowing the girls. This may not have been the best way to gather needed information, but in order to preserve the rather fragile balance of being both a woman and a researcher in a male-dominated culture, I did just that. With the teachers at Cobb High School, negotiating my role was an endless process. At the very worst I was considered as someone who was evaluating and reporting to the administrators what I observed. At the very best, I was someone who wanted to help. With each individual teacher, the process began anew as I conducted interviews or observed in the classroom.

In the community, the students called me "the White woman doing research." This was interesting because they are also White or Caucasian, but they considered themselves "Arab" and everyone else in the school was "White." I think that my presence was accepted and tolerated among these students, but I was not one of them, and they joked that perhaps I was a secret agent from the FBI or CIA spying on people. This was both a positive and negative aspect of the fieldwork. It was positive because it allowed me freedom to move about in the community without adhering to all the rules of modesty, although movement in the community was difficult because there was not a man (such as a husband or father) present to sanction my behavior. It was negative because the underlying assumption among my informants was that I would not understand them if I was not really Muslim as they were. As an outsider, I could never capture their reality. Wolf (1992) explains this dilemma and suggests that it *is* possible to capture that reality.

> Obviously (or so it seems to me), anthropologists can only convey their own understandings of their observations in another culture in their ethnographies. The better the observer, the more likely she is to catch her informants' understanding of the meaning of their experiences; the better the writer, the more likely she is to be able to convey that meaning to an interested reader from another culture. Some kinds of cultural meanings may only be accurately understood and reported by one who has learned them without realizing it, but much of the cultural onion *may* be easily or even more easily picked apart by a careful analyst who is not of the culture. (5)

I contacted the *hijabat* through the community center in the Southend and with the help of key contacts: Mrs. Dunbar, who worked at the community center, and two Yemeni American college students, Sabrina and Mariam. At first, contact with student participants was mediated by these key informants. Because the school district would not allow me to contact students through Cobb High School, I found a different venue for doing so. Dearborn is the home of the most successful Arab social services center in the United States. By contacting the youth and education director there, I was able to meet students who attended Cobb High and invite them to participate as focal students. Six *hijabat* agreed. They were tutors in a reading/writing program at the community center and helped newly arrived Arab immigrants (elementary and high school aged) with English and math. During the fall of 1997, I spent most of my afternoons at the community center getting to know the students. It soon became apparent to me that this was the only place other than school where I could possibly meet and speak with them. Although I was invited to parties and other social occasions in their homes in the ensuing few months, their home worlds remained relatively closed to me, although that began to change, as more of the students' mothers invited me to visit them. However, the community center served as a perfect and safe place for the *hijabat* to talk to me, and fieldwork at the high school officially began soon after.

The *hijabat* represented a range of ability and an array of dispositions toward their home and school lives. I interviewed them formally and informally and conducted participant observation in the community and school. Four additional participants included the only two Yemeni American *hijabat* from the community who were enrolled in college and the two Yemeni American boys. At the beginning I experimented with the idea of having a focal family and actually proceeded to interview one of my key informants and her two siblings. However, the parents refused to participate and the idea of a focal family became less important as other informants and their parents agreed to participate. At the high school, I formally interviewed twenty-two teachers and counselors over the two years of fieldwork and informally interviewed 75 of the 90 others. Teacher/counselor participants were chosen in accordance with student participants (their teachers), and teacher participation was voluntary and mediated by the district and school administration.

Participant and nonparticipant observation was conducted at school, in the community, and in the home. Focal students were shadowed at school, meaning that I followed them from the time they left their homes to the time that they returned home after tutoring at the community center. Artifacts such as schoolwork samples, personal work samples, community demographic information, daily bulletins, memoranda from district superintendent to and from principals, memoranda from principals to faculty, memoranda from the community liaison and media information were collected. Administrators at Cobb High were generous with their time and artifacts and let me photocopy whatever pertained to the Arab population in the school while I was there.

I was invited to homes on social occasions such as birthday parties and talked to mothers informally. Of course, all social occasions that took place in the home were with women, because men and women do not socialize together. In the school, I followed the six *hijabat* from class to class (and one time I shadowed one of the boys), all the while observing them and their interactions with the teachers, their peers, and the content taught. I conducted interviews with the teachers and attended staff meetings, Open House, school plays, school pep rallies, and a couple of football games.

At the community center, I conducted the interviews with the students and observed their interactions and language practices. I also participated in activities such as delivering food to poor and newly arrived Iraqi families during holidays, community center dinners, and reading/writing sessions with the tutors. In addition, the girls had a special group called Okhti (my sister). From time to time, this group met to talk about issues ranging from sexuality to school problems. It was important for me to continue these kinds of activities and to be seen as an integral part of the community. The informants all understood my research goals, but at the same time, they seemed to appreciate my participation in the work they did.

Several times I accompanied some of the *hijabat* to the nearby mall and to Arabic school at the mosque on weekends. Oftentimes, I would go to the mall by myself and walk there for a few hours, observing the various groups of people, especially when I knew that some of the Yemeni families had planned outings there. At Arabic school, I accompanied Nouria on either a Sunday or Saturday morning and observed first through seventh grades. The teachers there were suspicious of me at first but welcomed me back and were pleased to learn that I could read and write in Arabic, but they did suggest that I needed more Arabic language classes and said that I could enroll there.

I adopted the tools of ethnographic method—fieldnotes and ethnographic interviews—described by Emerson, Fretz, and Shaw (1995), Spradley (1979), and Hammersley and Atkinson (1995). A critical ethnographic analysis of the interviews included audiotaping, transcription, and coding based on domain, taxonomic, componential, and theme analyses (Carspecken 1996; Spradley 1979). By critical, I mean that I was especially aware of dialectical relationships such as power and gender, language and culture, and the politics of space, ethnicity, and class in my observations and the coding of fieldnotes. Observation fieldnotes were also analyzed through a process of open and focused coding in which I paid particular attention to the informants' use of culturally relevant terms and meaning making (Emerson, Fretz, and Shaw, 1995). I wrote analytical memos, which served two functions: they related the data to the formulation of theory, and they helped me gain analytical distance from the field itself (Miles and Huberman 1994; Strauss and Corbin 1990). In addition, a case study design (see Bogdan and Biklen 1992; Erickson and Shultz 1992) was used to document the discourse practices of each of the Yemeni students and to obtain a deeper and richer understanding of their day-to-day lives at home and at school. Attention to the particulars of each case illuminated the construction of their identities across contexts. Triangulation of codes and themes was applied among interviews, fieldnotes, and various artifacts. A constant application of member checks (with teachers, students, parents, and community members) across time was conducted. I did this by sharing ethnographic reports with administrators, teachers, and the girls. For example, I sent reports to Mrs. Dunbar to read, and I often called the *hijabat* on the weekends to read sections to them or to ask questions about my understanding of the Qur'an or other Arabic texts. Also, and importantly, during fieldwork, I met with two research mentors and colleagues once a month to discuss with them methodological issues as well as substantive ones dealing with my field experiences. These meetings guided me in not losing sight of my goals as I became more and more immersed in the Yemeni community.

*   *   *

The case of these Yemeni American girls and their community adds a unique lens to the history of immigration and education in the United States. As Suarez-Orozco (2001) reports, by 2020, one in every five students will be an immigrant or a child of immigrants. This certainly characterizes the Yemeni American girls of Dearborn and their progeny. Importantly, as relations between the United States and the Arab world continue to be highly politicized, and as ethnic and national identity becomes even more meaningful during moments of high tension in the world arena, the lives of these young women and their families at the end of the twentieth century and at the dawn of the twenty-first becomes all the more significant in our understanding of what it means to be a member of society, an American, an Arab, a Muslim, and a young woman. The world of public education is far more complicated than many of us know, especially for groups of people who are not active participants and consumers of the dominant and often hegemonic culture of schooling. This is the story of a group of high school girls who attempted to make sense of competing identities as their ethnic group was slowly becoming a majority group within their high school. As such, they present a compelling set of voices that show the determination and resilience of the contemporary American teenager in school, the Muslim daughters of the home and community, and the mothers of some of the United States' newest Arab and Muslim Americans.

Chapter 2

American Sojourners Between Honor and Shame

> A modern "ethnography" of conjectures, constantly moving between cultures, does not, like its Western alter ego "anthropology," aspire to survey the full range of human diversity or development. It is perpetually displaced, both regionally focused and broadly comparative, a form both of dwelling and of travel in a world where the two experiences are less and less distinct.

—James Clifford, *The Predicament of Culture*

There exists a strong relationship between the Yemeni American students and their land of origin. Layla, for instance, and the other *hijabat* and their families are sojourners, with one foot in the United States and the other in Yemen. This connection between their country of origin and their home in the United Statesis key to understanding these Muslim youths and their families.

The home world is much more than the physical space of a house in which the girls live. Home is not only a space; it is also a set of relationships and ideas that proffer a different set of expectations from those of school. The home world might mean living with parents and/or a husband and extended family, or it might simply mean the future possibility of a new home in either their U.S. community or Yemen. Importantly, home is really what the Yemeni American girls envision it to be and how they perceive its connection to school. As such, the notion of space becomes a relevant analytic tool for demarcating religious, ethnic, and gender boundaries. These boundaries, both social and physical, describe the spaces from which networks and identities emerge (Metcalf 1996). In other words, these spaces, whether they are religious (Muslim) or cultural (Yemeni and American), depict personal and community lives engaging with one another at multiple levels at different sites and on different continents. I examine the mechanisms for such engagement in the case of Layla and her Yemeni American peers, as I do the impact of these multiple spaces on their school lives.

Yemeni migration is part of a larger historical trend, as Arabs from the Middle East have immigrated to the United States for more than a century. The early Arab immigrants assimilated American cultural norms and the English language easily because they came from Judeo-Christian traditions and immigrated with the intent of making new lives for themselves and their children (Naff 1985, 1994). The most recent immigrants, those who have immigrated in the last twenty-five to thirty years, have typically been Iraqi or Yemeni and represent the "peasant" classes in their countries. Many moved to the Detroit area because they could find work in the large shipping and auto industries. Unlike earlier Arab immigrants, they have persisted in preserving both their Muslim ways of life and their Arab identities in the United States. Most of the Yemeni immigrants did not have any formal schooling in Yemen and are illiterate or semiliterate in Arabic and, in most cases, English. These immigrants have kept strong ties with their motherland, buying land in Yemen with the intention of going back, visiting for long periods, and sending their children there to marry. Consequently, in the United States, the children of these immigrants straddle two worlds, the literate world of school and the home world of religious and cultural values where text (the Qur'an) sanctions behavior, certain language use, disposition, and cultural norms.

Classic sociological theory maintains that a sojourner is one who remains attached to his or her own ethnic group while simultaneously living in isolation and staying apart from the host society. The sojourn itself is conceived as a "job" in which one travels back and forth during intervening years to the homeland (Siu 1952). Unlike a more common work schedule in which the worker returns home at least once a day, a sojourner may return home once a year or once in several years, and a successful sojourn, much like a successful job, entails sending money home to support one's family. While the notion of a sojourn as a job is compelling and commonly describes the migratory movement of immigrant populations in the United States, it is difficult to operationalize, especially when certain immigrant populations, such as the Detroit Yemeni, not only travel back and forth to Yemen but also settle in the United States. Most Yemeni enter the United States legally and become naturalized citizens and, importantly, settlers. Nonetheless, the notion of sojourner is a useful analytical tool in the case of Yemeni Americans because, as with most immigrant populations, the desire to return to the homeland remains pervasive among settlers. Yemeni Americans travel back and forth to Yemen often, and in the Detroit area, the Yemeni do, in fact, remain geopolitically, linguistically, religiously, and culturally isolated from American life while maintaining those same ties to their homeland.

Living in two worlds was both difficult and constraining for the Yemeni American Muslim girls. These students were academically successful in school, even as they struggled to negotiate their Yemeni and American selves in various contexts.[1] Their responsibilities were three-fold: to uphold the honor of the family, to become good mothers (most are engaged or married by the ages of 14 or 15 and earlier), and to succeed in school. In this chapter, I illustrate that these broadly defined responsibilities did not complement each other; rather, they created incongruities between the students' personal aspirations for success and their community's and/or school's demands for participation and learning in those respective contexts.

Making Space in the United States

In order to understand the lives of the six Yemeni girls and their peers in their community, it is important to understand the spaces they inhabited. Dearborn, a suburb of Detroit, had approximately ninety-five thousand residents during 1997–99. Because of its shipping and auto industries, Detroit and its suburbs have been a natural destination for immigrants seeking employment for more than one hundred years. Since the 1970s, southeastern Michigan, which includes the Detroit metropolitan area, has had the highest concentration of Arabic-speaking people outside of the Middle East—it was estimated that two hundred fifty thousand and more Arabic-speaking people resided there (Ameri and Ramey 2000; Zogby 1995). The Dearborn school district had a population of approximately 16,700 students in 1999, 49 percent of whom were Arabic speaking; 15 percent of these were of Yemeni origin. The Yemeni community resides about six and a half miles from the focal school site, Cobb High School.

Arab and non-Arab Americans consider Dearborn a nice place to live because of its low property taxes and its reputation for being "lily white" (Abraham, Abraham, and Aswad 1983), in contrast to Detroit, which is more than 80 percent African American and has considerable poverty and a lingering memory of the 1967 riots that contributed to its "White flight." The Yemeni community occupies a neighborhood in the Southend of Dearborn, where the Ford plant's smokestacks constantly spew dark clouds. Yemeni and Iraqi immigrants comprise most of the population of the Southend of Dearborn, while the Lebanese live in more affluent areas in and near Dearborn. Lebanese Americans constitute the majority of Arab Americans (about 41 percent) in Dearborn, whereas the Yemeni (about 18 percent) are the second largest group in the area. The median household income in the Southend of Dearborn is $20,125 (Zogby 1990, 1995). One-third of the population does not speak English, and many first-generation immigrant women are illiterate in their first language (Kulwicki 1987). Less than half of the population can both read and write English (Kuliwicki 1987). The Southend is a working-class community with two established mosques and several small coffee-houses. The mosques play a vital role in residents' lives, and the coffee-houses are traditional Middle Eastern social institutions in which men interact socially and politically. In some coffeehouses in Dearborn, a tra-ditional village hierarchy has been maintained and certain tables are reserved for the elderly village heads and avoided by the younger men (Abraham 1978; Abraham, Abraham, and Aswad 1983). The men dis-cuss community problems in the coffeehouses, and family feuds often surface there as well. These social institutions are distinguished both on the basis of nationality (e.g., Palestinian, Lebanese, or Yemeni) and by the particular village in the Middle East that the coffeehouse owner rep-resents. Virtually no women are ever seen on the streets of the Southend. The few Muslim women I observed on the streets in the area all wore the *hijab* and the *abaya* (a shapeless, ankle-length dress). Some Iraqi women covered their faces so that one could see only their eyes.

In 1997–99, the Dearborn school district included twenty-eight schools, three of which were high schools. Dearborn High School's stu-dents were predominantly White and middle to upper-middle class. Fin-kle High School's students were predominantly (approximately 75 percent) Arab American and of Lebanese origin. At least fifteen of Fin-kle's eighty teachers were Arab American. The students came from both working-class and middle-class families. Cobb High School, the school on which I focus, had approximately 1,420 students and ninety teachers. Of these students, 40 to 45 percent were Arabic speaking, and 41 percent of these were of Yemeni origin. During the 1998–99 aca-demic year, there were eleven Arabic-speaking teachers and staff, the majority of whom worked in the bilingual program, which mainly served newly arrived Yemeni and Iraqi immigrants. Cobb's mission was to be "committed to preparing [its] students to be responsible and well-informed."

Historically, Cobb High School began to receive students of Middle Eastern origin in the mid-1980s. Before that, it was a predominantly White school. I chose Cobb as the site for my study because, in making initial contact with the Yemeni community, I learned that the school and its students were experiencing difficulties adjusting to one another as the number of Arabic-speaking students increased. I wanted to learn more about how the school and students adapted to and accommodated one another in this site, that is, how the school and its teachers dealt with religious and cultural difference. Also the high school students who lived in the Southend were bused to Cobb rather than to Finkle High or Dearborn High, which were closer to the Yemeni community, and this created some discomfort in the Yemeni community.

In many ways, the Southend of Dearborn exists apart from the rest of the city. It is blocked from the rest of Dearborn by a wall of factories and smokestacks. The people who live there have formed their own cultural and linguistic spaces, traversing cautiously and usually through an intermediary, such as the local community center, which provides social, educational, and economic services.

While I lived in Dearborn, I rarely observed the *hijabat* alone in any context other than the centrally located community center, where the girls gathered as paid tutors from three to six each afternoon to work with mostly Yemeni elementary schoolchildren from the neighborhood. All of the girls in the Southend walked a block or so between the community center and their homes each day. On the weekends, they went shopping at the mall with their older brothers or married sisters, and/ or their parents. Whereas one might have seen non-Arab teenagers walking in groups throughout the mall, the Yemeni went out as families— going out to eat or shop was considered a family outing. Although this was always the case for the *hijabat,* boys had more freedom of movement farther away from the home, because parents tended to be more lenient with them. For example, many of the boys were allowed to work after school at the airport or in restaurants in downtown Detroit. Girls were rarely allowed to distance themselves from the home or to be seen in public working in what were considered to be male domains. Because public notice could ultimately lead to gossip and the loss of their good reputations, girls, if they worked at all, did so in the community center and rarely stepped outside the boundaries of the Southend. Girls left the Southend only to go to school or to go on family outings.

In the dynamic and lively Southend enclave, there was much visiting among the families who lived quite close to one another. Many of the houses were actually dual-family homes shared by two related families, or, in some cases, parts of the houses were rented out to newly arrived Yemeni boys and men from the owner's village in Yemen. People in the Southend tended to socialize with family members, such as cousins, or with people from the same village back home. There were two good reasons for this. First, dialects differ from village to village in Yemen. One of the girls told me that she and a nearby neighbor were not related and spoke different dialects. She explained, "We don't even understand each other when we talk—we're from different villages." Second, political alliances were important, and parents associated with people with whom they had connections in Yemen. This was useful for marriage purposes and for increasing one's status in the village upon returning to Yemen for a long-term stay. In effect, boys and girls lived in two very different worlds and by different rules at home and school; the distance from the Southend to Yemen appeared to be much closer than the six-and-a-half-mile distance from the Southend to Cobb High School.

The Influence of Yemeni Spaces in the United States

What connections with Yemen did the girls experience? How did these connections, this mingling of spaces within and outside the United States, impact their school lives? In order to answer these questions, it is worth considering migratory patterns within Yemen and from Yemen to the United States, for it is clear that life in the United States, particularly in the Southend, was often affected by events in Yemen. According to Molyneux (1998), a transitory period occurred between 1990 and 1994 when North Yemen (Yemen Arab Republic) and South Yemen (People's Democratic Republic of Yemen) were united into what we currently know as Yemen. Coincidentally, starting in 1985 and continuing through this period, the Southend received record numbers of Yemeni immigrants, mostly high-school-aged boys and young men. When Yemen became unified in 1990, South Yemen, which had had one of the most egalitarian secular codes in the Arab world, came under the heavy-handed and more religiously conservative influence of North Yemen. During the period between the British withdrawal from South Yemen in 1967 and Yemeni unification in 1990, South Yemen had adopted a "scientific socialism." Their family law explicitly stated the equality of men and women. In addition, free-choice marriage was established, with minimum marriage ages of sixteen for women and eighteen for men. Polygamy was prohibited except in cases of disease and barrenness, and bride price[2] was reduced from exorbitant amounts to 100 Riyal (approximately twice the average white-collar monthly salary) in 1974 (today, 150 Riyal ≈ $1). Both spouses would bear the cost of supporting their family, and unilateral divorce (*talaq*) by the husband was banned. Divorce could take place only in the courts, and men were not automatically given custody of the children.

North Yemen family law was different. In 1979, for example, polygamy was permitted, and the man had the right to unilateral divorce. Islamic law, or the *shari'a*, was the source of all laws as it had been for centuries. During the transition period of unification (1990–94), the family law was rewritten, and women's rights, according to Molyneux (1998), appeared in a section called "social problems" following sections devoted to illiteracy, tribal vengeance, and the use of the popular, mildly hallucinogenic narcotic *qat*. By 1992, Yemeni law had been revised to allow men four wives and to reduce the minimum marriage age for both men and women to fifteen. Forced marriages were illegal, but only women who had been married before had to give explicit consent—for previously unmarried women, silence could constitute consent. Marriage could be dissolved through the courts, but the husband had the unilateral right to divorce. A woman had the right to petition for divorce if her husband did not treat her as he did his other wives, if he was addicted to drugs or alcohol, if he refused to work, or if he was absent for a prolonged period. North Yemen's influence in South Yemen was made easier by the fact that South Yemen's more liberal laws had never been fully implemented and especially by the migration of North Yemeni men looking for work in South Yemen. Furthermore, families in South Yemen had protested against women's residential colleges, and Saudi Arabia had criticized South Yemen's "atheistic" legal reforms, especially the appointment of women judges in the family courts (Molyneux 1998). Control over bride price was no longer enforced, and it increased from 8,000–10,000 Riyal ($1,780 to $2,225) to 55,000–60,000 Riyal ($12,225 to $13,335) in the 1970s and 1980s (Stevenson and Baker 1991). All of these legal changes, in addition to civil war in the two Yemeni states, motivated men to travel elsewhere to find work and then return to buy land or to marry.

Although the Yemeni are relative newcomers to the United States, they have emigrated to other countries for centuries. Historically, North Yemen and, to some extent, South Yemen have depended on labor as their primary export. "The strategy based on remittances channeled back to the mother country continues to be at the heart of the labor-intensive migration for Yemenis," explains Friedlander (1998:ix). In fact, as much as one-fourth of the Yemeni male population emigrates, especially during times of political unrest, thus forcing Yemen to rely heavily on remittances, which account for one-third of Yemen's gross national product (Friedlander 1998). Money sent back to Yemen has been spent on consumer goods such as cars, VCRs, and inflated bride prices instead of long-term development of industry or better farming technology. As a result, men generally have tended to make long sojourns to work once the funds they brought back to Yemen from previous trips have been depleted. The women have been left behind to tend to the land and to farm *qat,* one of the most popular farm crops and a national pastime that is uniquely Yemeni within the Arab world.

Starting in 1975, families began to emigrate from Yemen to the United States (Friedlander 1998). According to the 1980 U.S. Census, at least twenty thousand Yemeni immigrated to Michigan, California, New York, and Ohio. Most of these immigrants came from North Yemen. The majority were men who, after a productive work period in the United

States, went back to their villages to give money, buy land, finance weddings, and build homes. In the late 1970s and early 1980s, some Yemeni men began to bring their families to the Southend because they found it to be a safe and inexpensive place, and the community center provided them all the services needed for settlement. The increase in the number of Yemeni families immigrating to the United States resulted in a growing Islamic conservatism, as men struggled to preserve their families' cultural integrity within American society (Swanson 1988). This increased conservatism in the United States mirrored that of North Yemen's influence on South Yemen, which also continued to be steadily influenced by Saudi Arabia, where many Yemeni men emigrated to work in the oil fields. Historically, Muslim men had been reluctant to bring their families to the United States (Naff 1985). For those Yemeni families who have remained in the United States, concern for their children's futures increased so that relationships between Yemen and the United States became closely maintained. Yemeni families have feared that American culture might have a negative impact on their children and their way of life. Swanson (1988) noted one such difference: "One difference between the American ethos and the Yemeni ethos is in the attitude toward moral responsibility. Americans emphasize that the individual is ultimately responsible for his own behavior. By contrast, Yemeni culture insists that it is the community that is responsible for evolving a social and political system that at once protects the individual from temptation and ensures his conformity to group values (63)."

In Dearborn, the Yemeni took control of the mosque from the Lebanese community in the Southend, and with funding for the mosque from Saudi Arabia, they struggled to maintain traditional, cultural, and religious norms, especially among the youth. Barth (1969) observes that a person's maintenance of an ethnic identity depends upon both the perceived advantages of membership in the ethnic group and one's ability to perform his or her ethnic role. Invariably, it was to the Yemeni girls' advantage to maintain cultural mores in the Southend, otherwise the consequences were dire. The loss of one's good reputation resulted in parents pulling their daughters out of school, forcing an early marriage, and sending them to Yemen. Sometimes, in grave situations in which the family's honor was at stake, fathers and brothers killed their daughters/sisters (Aswad and Bilgé 1996). For the boys, many of whom lived with extended family members while their parents remained in Yemen, life in the United States meant an opportunity to earn money and send it back home. Unlike the boys, girls always lived with their parents, and the girls about whose lives I write here either were born in the United States or emigrated from Yemen at a very young age (infant to age four). In general, for both boys and girls, being Yemeni and American was problematic, but especially for the girls, whose good reputation rein-forced a family's status both in the Southend and in their home village in Yemen.

Layla's story in particular illustrates the irreconcilability of the spaces she and the other *hijabat* inhabited. It is possible that, in two or three generations, American youth of Yemeni or Arab origin will not experi-ence such tension or the intensive and constant negotiation of home, school, and "old-country" worlds. But the Yemeni girls lived lives full of uncertainties, not knowing whether they would finish high school or get married, go to Yemen or perhaps attend college. In all likelihood, the girls would marry early. The early marriage of daughters and sons to Yemeni nationals (although boys were usually not married as early as girls) allowed these Arab families to preserve and maintain their ethnic-ity. The advantages of such marriages were threefold. First, young men from Yemen obtained U.S. residency and were able to send remittances to their families, thus continuing Yemen's successful economic depen-dence on emigration. Second, particular family or village affiliations grew larger in the Southend through marriage, bringing increased status and wealth to the family on both continents and ensuring that the girls were supported financially. Third, religious and cultural traditions were, to a large extent, reproduced—for example, Arabic remained the language of the home because one of the spouses was usually illiterate in English and/or print-illiterate in Arabic and English. Under such cir-cumstances, the girls from the Southend grew up remarkably fast. In light of these governing factors, Ogbu's (1982a, 1982b, 1993) cultural-ecological model is useful for understanding what is required for adap-tation and the successful realization of cultural mores. In his view, child rearing in the family and subsequent adolescent socialization aim at developing instrumental competencies required for adult economic, political, and social roles. His model is relevant here because it helps explain that the *hijabat* had to learn to be competent housekeepers and students at an early age in order to facilitate the lives of their parents and their spouses. Portes and Rumbaut's (1996) concept of dissonant acculturation is especially salient here too. They argue that when par-ents lack sufficient education or integration into the community in which they live, they must depend on their children's guidance to cope with the outside environment. They explain that generational disso-nance "occurs when second generation acculturation is neither guided nor accompanied by changes in the first generation" (241). In Layla's case, regardless of the events that occurred outside her home culture, she still had to learn to become Yemeni (albeit displaced) in the same manner her parents were Yemeni and at the same time provide them the support and guidance they needed to survive in the American world.

Consequently, because the *hijabat* shared their parents' lives, they were also sojourners, with each foot planted in a different space. Even the intimate spaces of domestic and ritual life, meaning, and behavior were shaped by the contexts of the larger society.

The Case of Layla: A Representative Portrait

Over two years, I learned a great deal about Layla and her family. We communicated at school, at the community center, at parties and weddings, and by written correspondence and telephone when I was away from Dearborn. I interviewed her mother and met all of her friends in different contexts, such as in the mosque during Arabic school and at Cobb High School and in the "Ramadan room," where all the Muslim students fasted during the holy month. Layla's story is not unique; it is similar to those of the other girls in Dearborn, when I knew her as a tenth and eleventh grader. In fact, Layla's experiences are similar to that of another Yemeni American woman who published a poignant account of her life in Dearborn: "As soon as we walked over the threshold into our house, we walked into Yemen. . . . In this Yemeni world, I had a certain role to play based on my gender" (Alwujude 2000:384–85). Layla's story is the *hijabat*'s story and illustrates concretely their negotiation of the two worlds they inhabited, and especially their roles in relation to their villages in Yemen and their families in Dearborn.

Layla was a sojourner. She wanted to live in the United States, but she liked going to Yemen because her family enjoyed a high status as Americans while there. In many ways, Layla and the Yemeni American girls lived in suspense, not knowing which space they were likely to inhabit in the near future. Layla navigated multiple spaces and found a "home" in managing the liminal spaces she occupied. It was not always clear to her whether she was American or Yemeni, and her attitude toward her home and school lives reflected her consternation with both identities. Undeniably, she was a Yemeni Muslim, and her Muslim space, governed by ritual and sanctioned practice, permitted a view of the world that was not always satisfying to a young adolescent girl with dreams for a bright future and with exposure to alternative images of what she could become.

Layla and the other *hijabat* experienced a primary affiliation with their Yemeni family, village, Arabs in general, and their religion. Their secondary affiliation was with "America." However, the boundaries were not very clear, for America was their country while Yemen was their *imagined* homeland, at least until they traveled there to visit or to marry. For the girls, the sojourn was really a feeling of impermanence, a disembodiment with the local environment and a simultaneous intellectual and emotional connection with a familial origin. Layla, like all the other Yemeni American students, identified herself as Yemeni, Arab, and American, in that order. She thought of herself, as the other *hijabat* did, as Arab and not "White," a category reserved for "Americans." Both of her parents were "Yemeni, just like me," even though she was born in the United States. Her father was born in "the village" in North Yemen where there were few work or educational opportunities. He arrived in the United States in the late 1960s at the age of sixteen and worked in the auto factories. Her mother was born in the city of Aden, the old capital of South Yemen, and lived alongside the British. She arrived in the United States in the 1970s with Layla's older brothers. Layla's parents were an unusual couple—they were not cousins, and one of them was from a city and from the South, which most northern Yemenis considered lower status and too liberal. Layla's parents met through common family friends in Yemen and lived in relative social and economic security among their North Yemeni neighbors in the Southend. Layla's father worked at the Ford River Rouge Plant. Her mother did not work outside the home, though she volunteered for a while at the elementary school a few blocks away from their home in the Southend, monitoring the playground during recess. Layla's parents had some elementary education in Yemen. Her mother went through sixth grade in the city and had been exposed to English. Both parents had minimal fluency in English (they did not read, write, or speak much English) and minimal print fluency. In my interviews with Layla and in my observations of her in Arabic school, Layla made it clear that she was a fair reader and speaker of Arabic, but her writing ability was minimal. Layla's family income was about $1,200–$1,600 per month. Her two older brothers, both in their mid- to late twenties, attended college and worked at jobs away from the neighborhood.

Layla tried to avoid marriage to her first cousin from Yemen. Marriages were important events in the Southend. They signified a girl's coming of age, a time during which her role as a Yemeni woman rather than a high school girl was reinforced. During the 1997–98 school year, which was her sophomore year, Layla's family spent six months in Yemen visiting relatives. During that time Layla was engaged to be married, and upon her return she attempted to keep her marriage engagement a secret from her friends. Nonetheless, many learned the information from her father, who was proud of this future union because this first cousin (from her father's side) was a *sayyid*, a direct descendent of the prophet Muhammad. Her father told most of the community about the engagement. Her prospective husband would pay a bride price of 200,000 Riyal (approximately $1,333 in 1999), but Layla believed that she was worth much more. Layla's consternation with her prospective bride price depicts a dilemma many of the Southend *hijabat* faced. On the one hand, they were highly educated and literate in comparison to their Yemeni husbands. On the other hand, their being American characterized them as riskier mates than women born and reared in Yemen. Hence, bride price was sometimes adjusted to reflect this risk. In addition, it is possible that bride price was lowered in anticipation of the costs the men would incur in their move to the United States.

In the Southend, a marriage was not consummated immediately, but the *ahked* (loosely translated as a binding betrothal of marriage) took place in Yemen, and in the United States this constituted a legal marriage. Layla never discussed her engagement at school. She wanted to avoid marriage to her twenty-year-old cousin—a young man she said she had not seen since their return from Yemen—because she knew that marrying one's first cousin was "bad" in the United States. Her fiancé worked in a factory in Dearborn and did not live with her family. Layla insisted that she had considered marriage to him so that the young man could enter the country as a legal U.S. resident. Helping cousins or village friends from Yemen enter the United States was often a byproduct of marriage for many of the girls. Unfortunately for many of the girls, they could not obtain a legal U.S. divorce while their husbands awaited their naturalization papers. And in fact they could not initiate divorce proceedings at all because, as was the custom in Yemen and in the Southend, only the man had the right to *talaq*, or unilateral divorce. To bypass immigration restrictions, the *hijabat* were willing to travel back to Yemen, have their husbands declare the divorce,[3] and quickly return to the United States and worry about a legal divorce at a later time. In other words, the girls were much more concerned with the Islamic laws governing their marriages than with the U.S. laws that bound them legally to their husbands.

Some of the Yemeni girls in the Southend were reluctant to admit that they were married. They were very careful not to be seen associating with their husbands at school or in the community. This would validate their Yemeni marriages even further, and they did not want to be identified as married when there was the chance that they would divorce. Also, being seen with their husbands might destroy their reputations because the marriage had not been consummated. Nouria, another of the *hijabat*, confessed that she had done everything—from insulting her husband to asking him to talk to her father directly—to "get him to divorce [her]," but nothing had worked. Layla was not as forceful, but she wanted to avoid marriage. At the same time, she did not want to disappoint her family. The possible marriage union between her family and her cousin's family was a difficult one to break, especially because his family was related to hers through her father. Marriage for these girls was an unsettling process, but there was often no exit once the *ahked* took place.

Marriage was in many ways an obstacle to the girls' future goals. The institution of marriage brought to the surface cultural tensions that were not easily reconciled in the Yemeni girls' American spaces. Layla recognized that girls in the United States have more opportunities than do those in Yemen. A Yemeni friend who was a 4.0 student told her, "I really don't want to go to high school no more 'cause I know my mom, my parents won't let me go to college." This depressed Layla, who was a good student herself, and it made her angry because her friend was intelligent and had a bright future ahead of her. "And that's what makes me mad," she emphasized, "we're not like the girls in Yemen. We have a chance to do something with our lives and they just wanna think, oh, no. You're going to get married and do this. That's not how it is. I mean, I would never do that to my kids." In Yemen, according to Layla, even though she considered it to be "a primitive place," a good education was respected. Many women regretted not going to college, and "a lot of them wanted to do something with their lives." Layla had a cousin in Yemen, for example, whose father stopped her from going to school in the sixth grade even though she wanted to continue. Now, at twenty-one, Layla's cousin wanted to train to become a seamstress so that she could at least make a living sewing clothes for people. Layla could not come to terms with her cousin's situation; it seemed somehow alien, even though it reflected her own fears for her future during and after her last year of high school. Later, when I interviewed Layla in February 2002, she informed me that she had avoided marriage and was traveling often with her family to Yemen to visit relatives and friends.

Despite its minor role in Yemen, education was important, perhaps as important as marriage, to the Yemeni community in the Southend.[4] Although the parents of the *hijabat* had not received much formal schooling, they took seriously their daughters' and sons' education. They sent their children to public school and to Arabic school on the weekends—most of the Yemeni children in the community attended school seven days a week.[5] At the same time, however, the Southend community feared the social aspects of public schooling and limited their children's experiences there. Social life in school was monitored and curtailed by family members. "She's supposed to be quiet, walk in the halls like nobody knows her," Layla explained the girl's role in school. Layla's brothers told her not to hang out with the "loud ones, the ones who always laugh, the ones who always play around." If Layla was too loud, then people would say that she was trying to draw attention from the boys. This was a common thread in all the girls' interviews and in my observations of school life.

School life for the Yemeni girls involved crossing and recrossing various religious, cultural, and gender boundaries. Certain classes, such as gym, caused anxiety and frustration among the Yemeni girls, an anxiety mirrored by their parents. The girls requested their own gym classes with a female teacher, but, because of the lack of space, they still shared the same gym with the boys. The girls worried about being seen in T-shirts, and Layla said that she did not feel right when a boy watched her as she ran on the track or inside the gym. Her arms showed and her chest jiggled, she said. She commented that at lunch in the cafeteria the school accepted who they were—the girls went their way and the boys went theirs. In class, socializing with boys was fine because they talked about schoolwork; elsewhere it did not feel right, and in gym it was wrong. Sabrina, one of two *hijabat* in the Southend community attending college at the time, clarified Layla's uneasiness with gym class: "A sport is jumping and running and doing. . . . A girl should be, because of the way I'm raised and the way it is, you know, a girl is supposed to sit, you know, legs crossed." Although only three semesters of gym were required at Cobb, some girls enrolled in the class for four years, failing it each time because they did not dress in gym clothes or participate in class. This situation was exasperating for both them and their teachers.

The gendering of common spaces by both Yemeni boys and girls was reinforced at home and school. For example, when Layla was required to take technical education, her brothers questioned her about it because it was not a "girl's class." They did not want her to take auto shop either. She enrolled in the same classes, such as homemaking or clothing, as her *hijabat* friends. One of Layla's best friends, Aisha, a high achiever, refused to take classes in which she was the only girl who wore the scarf; she dropped them and took other ones. The Yemeni boys generally stayed out of classes such as clothing or homemaking, as did almost all of the boys at Cobb High. These were girls' spaces, and as a teacher observed, these classes were the only places in the school where the Arab girls sometimes felt safe enough to remove their scarves.

Ironically, school was still an actively social place for the *hijabat*, even when they experienced cultural tensions between American-Yemeni and female-male spaces. Layla reported that she liked school because she socialized with friends; school was one of the few places where all the girls could see one another. But, she admitted, there were grudges and prejudice between Arabs and non-Arabs. She alluded to a food fight that occurred the previous year and to insults and name-calling traded between the boys. Layla distinguished her "American friends" from her Yemeni friends by levels of connection and comfort: "[My friends] are all Yemeni because that's who I like. You know, I like to hang around with my, the people that I really connect with."

In addition to family concerns about school and its potential negative social influences, the *hijabat* lived under the constant watch of Yemeni boys. Reminiscent of Foucault's (1977) famous panopticon, the gaze of these boys often altered the girls' behavior, especially in the hallways, in the cafeteria, and during after-school activities.[6] The gaze, and the girls' perception of the gaze, shifted in accordance with their location in and out of school. For example, before going to Yemen, Layla had been involved in a few extracurricular activities such as International Club, but none that took place after school. She found that life could be frustrating at school when the girls participated in extracurricular activities. One of Layla's friends, a Yemeni American girl who did not wear the *hijab*, wanted to run track.[7] When the Yemeni boys found out that she wanted to join the track team, they began to spread rumors about her. "They don't want us to do anything!" Layla exclaimed. The Yemeni boys at Cobb had a subtle but potent surveillance role—they were the ones who reported girls as having bad reputations to parents and the community. Bad reputations consisted of certain behaviors, such as being too loud, talking with boys, and participating in after-school activities. Most of the Yemeni girls at school, as in Foucault's description of prison inmates, internalized the threat they perceived from the boys' gazes and changed their behavior accordingly. The *hijabat* were quiet and kept their distance from the boys as much as possible. The married girls especially feared the false rumors that could reach their husbands, who would have the right to threaten their wives' personal safety and take them out of school.

A wave of religious conservatism swept through the Southend in the 1980s and 1990s, paralleling the political situation in North Yemen and the Middle East. Layla observed that the boys and the parents in the neighborhood had grown very strict, always watching the goings-on of the girls. "Nobody trusts anybody for some reason," she tried to explain. It was her understanding that in Yemen people "behaved normally," while in the United States everyone "got the wrong idea" and said "people are going to talk about you." According to Layla, although the women were usually covered from head to toe in Yemeni villages, they still interacted with men around mundane household and village tasks without worrying about the consequences of being seen. At the mosque, during the Arabic school for girls only, Layla and the girls were told by the teachers to look down when they walked in the hallways of the Dearborn public schools; otherwise, boys would look directly in their eyes and have evil thoughts. When Layla entered high school her life changed. "I came into high school and everybody told me you gotta do this, you gotta do this, you gotta do this and this in order to live a happy life in high school. And that was don't look at guys, don't talk to guys, don't laugh loud in the hallways, don't socialize a lot in the hallways. Just keep up the education." These types of messages and "surveillance" intensified at Cobb High School because it was so much farther away from the Southend than the middle schools had been, and community members and parents experienced a loss of control when their daughters were bused almost ten miles away. There also had been a history of high school *hijabat* who had misbehaved with boys, and parents worried about this (Aswad and Bilgé 1996). Layla did not associate with boys unless the talk was about homework. One example she related to me in her worries about associating with boys was about a girl who ran away and married an African American boy from Detroit who was not a Muslim. Her parents had had a Yemeni boy from Yemen in mind for her. This incident frightened the whole community, which became suspicious of anything over which they did not have control. School yearbooks, for instance, became an issue of control among all of the Yemeni girls and their families following the incident of the runaway girl. During conversations over lunch in the cafeteria, Layla and other *hijabat* informed me that boys would cut out girls' photos and tell everyone that "so and so is my girlfriend." This caused parents to worry about their daughters' reputations, and they prevented many girls from having their photos taken for the yearbook. This incident was followed by the publication of a pamphlet, "Awareness." It was written by one of the Yemeni high school boys and was passed around. The pamphlet included (in Layla's words) "that a girl holds the family's name. She reflects on her family and the parents have a hold on her. She can't be a 'ho' [whore]; otherwise it reflects badly on the parents. Girls shouldn't listen to American music on the school buses, especially to songs that are sexually explicit." Layla keenly observed that when the girls were so controlled by others, they tried to break away and often chose the wrong way, such as talking to and forming relationships with boys or disregarding their Yemeni community, parents, and friends. As a result, parents married off their daughters early to men from Yemen.

The spaces within which Yemeni girls lived their lives were often closely scrutinized by the Yemeni community. School was not the only place that was worrisome to the Yemeni families in the Southend. Any space outside the home was questionable, at least for the girls and women. For Layla, life centered on her home and nearby surroundings. Her younger sister walked the few blocks to attend Arabic school with all the neighborhood girls. Her mother usually stayed home. Only her brothers and her father left the vicinity of the house when they went to work. Layla tutored at the community center a few blocks from her home and handed her earnings to her parents, who maintained houses in the Southend and in Yemen. She was allowed to work at the community center because her friend and next-door neighbor Aisha did, and her mother trusted this particular friend and her family. Layla explained, "She [Aisha] has a clean rep. She [Layla's mother] thinks she's a very good girl. My mom has a lot of trust in me because of the friends I have." In other words, Layla's activities were limited to what the "good" girls in the neighborhood did. This satisfied her parents' safety concerns and ensured that everyone knew she was behaving properly.

Layla's and her mother's social lives revolved around their nearby relatives and neighbors, whom they visited often. Layla usually went out shopping or to a neighbor's house with Aisha and Aisha's married sister. The girls were not allowed to go to movies, and most of them had never been inside a movie theater. Movie theaters posed a threat: "The room is dark and people do bad things in there, like making out," Layla explained. When Layla went to a movie, she had to go with someone of whom her parents approved. For example, Layla was allowed to see the movie *Titanic* because she went with Sabrina and Mariam, two older "good" girls in charge of the tutors at the community center. "I'd be allowed to go because Mariam, she lives right next to me, too, and my parents, they're like, she's a really good role model. You know, because she's in college, you know, she drives a car and she has a job." As Layla's description of different physical spaces illustrates, Mariam's proximity to Layla's family and her good reputation (as one of the two Southend Yemeni girls in college at the time) played an important role in her parents' decision to allow Layla to participate in an activity away from home. The same held true for all the girls in the study. They tended to be involved as a group when they participated in activities outside the home so that there was no question of inappropriate behavior or concerns for the girls' safety. Importantly, the group consisted of girls whose reputations were above reproach and whose families had high-status (religious and economic) positions in the community.[8]

As with all the Yemeni girls, Layla had many chores to do at home, in part to prepare for her own home and marriage. Learning how to do housework and how to cook at an early age served two functions. First, most Yemeni families in the Southend had at least four children, sometimes seven to twelve children, and the older girls were needed to help around the house. Second, because the girls were usually married at an early age, between twelve and fifteen, they were expected to know how to care for their own homes in the future. Layla, for example, cleaned as soon as she arrived home from school and after she worked at the community center. During the weekends, she learned how to cook with her mother, and all the cousins were invited for family dinners. Other Yemeni girls reported similar activities. As one of the other *hijabat*, Amani, said, "I have more home responsibilities now. I have to do more cooking. My mom expects me to know how to do things for the future. Ladies come over and look me over, look my cooking over. It's a lot of pressure." Like Layla, Amani was expected to perform well in the kitchen and at home, for it was likely that she would be married to one of the visiting ladies' relations. As Layla grew older, her mother spent more time teaching her how to cook Yemeni dishes. "She's accepting me more as a lady, more grown up. She's respecting my privacy for one thing," Layla said about her mother. Layla felt that she was more of a woman than a girl and that her mother's treatment of her had changed accordingly. She included Layla in decision making, asked her for advice or information, and took her along when shopping or visiting friends. Her brothers stopped wrestling with her as they used to do. Now the siblings had serious conversations. Although Layla understood the changes that were occurring, she did not accept them willingly. Her mother often compared her to other girls who cleaned the whole house and who could cook a whole dinner, whereas Layla had yet to make an entire meal. Layla was methodical, whereas her mother could do several things at the same time. Her mother often grew impatient if she perceived her daughter to be avoiding housework or homework. "I'm like children of America," Layla would say, alluding to the fact that her American self was rebelling against what she perceived as Yemeni responsibilities and missed opportunities:

I mean, since I'm raised here—in like Yemen, they're so primitive. That's how I look at it. I mean, primitive is a really old, old word to use. I mean, but they are. I mean, they just don't wanta let go of the fact that, you know, this is the twentieth century, going on to the twenty-first, you know. "People: things have changed and you have to accept it!" And I didn't, they just like, these people, I mean, my parents are okay. I mean, compared to other parents, I'm like, it really makes me mad because, first of all, their daughters have a good, they have like doors open for them. They have a huge opportunity. You know, more than the girls in Yemen that they wish they could do. Do you know what I mean?

The Yemeni girls from the Southend shouldered a great deal of responsibility at a young age. They had to excel in all domains of their lives—school, home, and housekeeping—in preparation for marriage. These responsibilities took their toll, making school a burden for some rather than a means for social and intellectual development and mobility. When Layla reached her junior year of high school, she decided to take school more seriously because she was worried about her future and what she would be able to accomplish. She focused more on her studies and less on her friends, and she noticed that her teachers were also focusing more on preparing students for college. Doing well in school increased the likelihood that her parents would allow her to attend college. Layla had to prove to her parents that she could improve her 3.0 grade point average from the previous year. Her grades could become her ticket to college, otherwise there would not be much hope of her going. Layla observed that many of the Arab girls gave up in high school: "they wasted four years of their lives when they said that they were going to be married." She claimed that the Arab girls got lazy in school, knowing that they could not go to college, "so what's the point of trying?" She wanted to prove to her friends that they could go by going herself. She paid attention to her teachers, who had told her that she was a good student, an overachiever. Layla liked to hear this praise because she struggled with her home responsibilities and expectations: "Well, today my, my teacher was telling me that I'm an overachiever. That's what he told me. That made my day, and a lot of other teachers, they're like, 'You know, you're doing a good job. I can see that you're really trying to work hard.' Yeah. I'd love to be an historian. I think it's cool to dig up old stuff and . . . try to figure out, you know, mysteries, and I think it's cool. But I don't know. Like I was telling my mother about it and she was just like, you know, 'I doubt you're gonna be that.'"

At times, Layla was confused and unhappy with her situation at home. She preferred to be at school. One cause of her unhappiness was her father's use of *qat*, a plant grown in Yemen where it is a legal narcotic, but its use is illegal in the United States. Like many men and women in Yemen, Layla's father invited his male friends to his house where they sat in a room whose perimeter was covered by mattresses. They discussed political issues, smoked a tobacco pipe, and chewed *qat*, which produces a mild euphoria. In Yemen as in the Southend, chewing *qat* is an important social activity—*qat* parties are arenas for announcing news and reinforcing social status (Stevenson and Baker 1991). In fact, the farming of *qat* and coffee make up 10 percent of all cultivated land in Yemen. Religious authorities sanction *qat*, but the Yemeni government opposes it because it is considered a health hazard, a drain on household budgets, and an obstacle to economic development, because *qat* parties may start at one in the afternoon and continue into the evening. Nevertheless, the Yemeni government profits considerably from the production and marketing of *qat* (Varisco 1986). For Layla's family, *qat* was a large expense—one *rubta*, or bundle, for a day of chew cost between fifteen and twenty dollars—which made life harder for them. With all the family expenses in Yemen and in the Southend, including *qat*, life, Layla noted, was not "what it used to be." Layla's family was building a house in Yemen, so that project along with the expense of *qat* drained the household budget. Layla preferred going to school where she could be with Yemeni friends who understood her problems and with whom she could talk. "They make me feel like really happy. I have friends that have to deal with the same issue . . . they deal with the same things," she said.

Home life was complicated further by what Layla perceived to be a gender bias in the Yemeni community. Her mother wanted her to go to college, but her father pushed marriage. Layla was often angry that girls in Yemen were taken out of school during their elementary years. "They're not given the freedom of choosing education," she insisted. Layla argued that if she was not going to have a choice about going to college, she might as well stop school now. She maintained that parents felt differently about education for boys and girls: "A guy is supposed to have an education because he's the only thing that can hold a family together; he'd feel low if he depended on his wife for money." Sometimes Layla thought this was simply the way things were. "Like, if you're lucky to graduate [from high school], you know, good for you, but you still gotta go home to the kitchen." At least, that is what her aunt always told her. The girls did not go to college; Mariam and Sabrina were exceptions among the Yemeni young women in the Southend. The boys went to college unless they had families to support, although college was more of an option if it resulted in a better paying job. If Layla had been able to do anything she wanted in the world, she would have gotten "rid of the boys at school because they stress[ed] the girls out so much." She stated plainly that she wanted to be rid of all the selfish and foolish guys that made girls uncomfortable. "You know, it's like you can never trust a person. You never know what they'll do to you," she added. She thought that the boys had been given too much freedom, much more than the girls, because the attitude was that boys could take care of themselves. Layla noted that because girls were thought to be more vulnerable, they were expected to cover themselves, especially if they were attractive. Layla saw herself going to college, becoming a nurse, a teacher, a pharmacist, a historian, or a politician, but she doubted she could become a politician because, "being an Arabic girl," she could not go into something that is "supposedly a man's job." As it turned out, the *hijabat* and most of the Yemeni American girls with whom I spoke in the high school and at parties hoped to become nurses and teachers, vocations they thought would go hand in hand with motherhood and their future home lives.

Perhaps the most troubling issue for Layla and other Yemeni girls was the question of the return to Yemen. Yemen had changed for the better, and her parents wanted to return there, especially Layla's mother. She was happy in the United States at first, but no longer. Layla emphasized her parents' sojourn mentality: "They come here, looking for work, and as soon as they're retired, they just go back because they see nothing else for them here. What else, they're just gonna live in poverty over here. So they just go back to their own homeland and they'll be like respected so much and they'll receive a check for $1000, like every month. So, they'll be living like the middle class here in Yemen." Several of the Southend families wanted to return to Yemen where their retirement pensions would place them solidly in the middle or upper-middle class and where they would enjoy a higher social status. Most of the girls did not want to leave the United States, however. At school they saw that the "boaters" (as in "right off the boat," a pejorative term used at Cobb High to denote new immigrants and others who do not conform to particular social norms, such as wearing the right shoes) were Yemeni boys who, like their fathers, came to the United States because there was nothing for them in Yemen. According to Layla, these boys came from the villages, the lower classes, and were uneducated. When they arrived in the United States, they could not believe all the girls and women they saw outside the home who were so openly uncovered and did not relate well to this change. Layla was afraid of becoming part of that village life in Yemen. She liked traveling to and being in Yemen with her parents as members of the upper classes, "who are more sophisticated and have interesting conversations." She enjoyed the high status of being an American Yemeni in Yemen. However, she did not want to be married to a village man who did not have that status.

Once in a while, when Layla purposefully forgot that she was engaged, she fantasized about having a boyfriend. When she saw people walking hand in hand in the school hallways or at the mall, she could not wait to be married to the man she would choose so that she could hold his hand. Instead, Layla was expected to go with her family to Yemen after she graduated from high school. Her father wanted to retire there because their house was built. She was afraid of making this journey and being unable to return to the United States or go to college. She did not want marriage unless "[she] fell in love with a millionaire or something." For Layla, the journey to Yemen was fraught with anxiety, for she had no control over events in which she played a central, albeit silent, role.

The return to Yemen was marked by the imposition of cultural norms, which grew steadily more frequent as the Yemeni girls matured. Layla's father, for instance, had a strong influence on her behavior and dress. He told her when she entered the third grade that she had to wear the *hijab* because other girls did. He also wanted her to wear an *abaya* (a long-sleeved shapeless dress), but Layla insisted on wearing loose jeans and large, long-sleeved shirts. Sometimes she wore a long skirt. Upon her family's return from Yemen during Layla's tenth grade year, her father identified her with the women from Yemen, suggesting that Layla had finally learned who she really was: "And then he'll tell me . . . 'now that you went to Yemen, you see how we are, why don't you just wear like a, you know, an *abaya?*'" Layla explained that her father was used to seeing women wearing *abayas* and covering their hair in the house. During Layla's stay in Yemen during that school year, she wondered why she had to wear the *hijab* in the house when men were not present. Her mother never dressed that way in the early 1970s when she lived in Aden shortly after British colonialism ended. Layla thought she related better to her mother's "society," the city life, as opposed to her father's "village life." "I really, I relate to my mother and I really don't accept my father's kind of living," she said. Layla commented that her father did not know that there was a difference between there and here: "He still doesn't accept it." Yet Layla had to contend with the cultural norms of her imagined and very real homeland, and as she grew older those became more explicit and less flexible.

Layla was not alone in experiencing inconsistencies between her American and Yemeni lives. All of the girls struggled with these issues every day, as did some of the boys. Layla's brother, for instance, married his first cousin in Yemen. According to Layla, they were not close cousins. In the Yemeni patrilineal society, marrying someone from the mother's side meant that blood ties were not as strong. "In our tradition, you're more closer to your dad's side than you are to your mother's side," Layla explained. The idea that a mother's line was not as strong as a father's was disturbing to the girls, especially when they learned in biology class that this was, from a scientific perspective, wrong. Countless times during my fieldwork, the *hijabat* would ask if marrying a cousin was healthy. Layla worried incessantly about being married to her first cousin on the father's side, the "closer side." The girls were confused by what they learned about genetics at school and what they knew of their own cultural traditions. Aisha, for instance, revealed that her own parents were first cousins and that one of her siblings had died at a young age from some type of physical handicap. Yet, in the end, the girls tended to accept their parents' decisions about marriage, no matter what doubts they had at the intersection of their two cultures.

Layla had very clear ideas about what it meant to be Yemeni and what it meant to be American. To her, Yemeni meant wanting to get married; American meant wanting to go to college. "I want to be able to do what my parents want because I want to please my parents, you know. But at the same time, you know, I can't 'cause it's not something that's in my heart," Layla reported. One of her goals was to finish high school and go on to college, but she knew that her family did not support the idea. She made the point that she was Muslim, too, but to her that was a matter of faith and not culture. To please her parents she read the Qur'an every night, and her parents were very proud of her for getting through the whole text and all of the prayers. However, she maintained that she did not think she could balance a marriage and pregnancy with college. In Yemeni culture, having children was central in perpetuating the image of a good woman, and pregnancy could not be avoided. Knowing this, Layla was under pressure to earn good grades at the end of her junior year. If there was a chance for her to attend college, it was by showing her parents that she was a good student in high school. "That's kind of why I'm trying to do as good as I can 'cause I know years are going, flying by," she explained. Her brothers were not supportive of her efforts; they thought she should stay at home and cook, and they told her that their mother needed help in the house. They forbade her to go to college. For Layla, being a girl at home was not easy. College represented far more than an education for her, as it did for many of the Yemeni girls who wanted such an opportunity. College meant solidifying their American space:

> I don't like it when I see Arabic girls, all they think about, they joke around but at the same time, they take it [college] seriously. You know, "Oh, what are we gonna do after high school?" Well, they're like, "We're gonna get married, you know." That doesn't necessarily have to happen. You know, you don't have to just get married. And what's the whole point? You lost four years of your life in high school, you just wasted it. What's the point? And I wanta prove to other girls that, you know, you're able to go to college. You're in America. You can do this.

College was also an avenue to liberation from certain constraints that no longer made sense to Layla either in Yemen or in the Southend. She commented that women in Yemen who have college degrees are respected: "[There's] lots of respect because, like I said, like some ladies, they'll be like, 'Oh, she's going to college.' And then there's some ladies, 'Oh, look, she wants to do something. She's not just gonna sit home and do, you know, just cook and get married.' Because some, a lot of them regret not going to college. A lot of them wanted to do something with their lives." Doing something with one's life (other than maintaining a household) was important to Layla. Her notion of liberation—going to college—meant that the physical, economic, and gendered spaces imposed by her culture would have to change. To her and other *hijabat*, this was possible as long as they maintained good grades and good reputations in the United States.

Sojourning into a New Space

The Yemeni girls in the Southend were proud of their Yemeni culture, religion, and traditions, yet they also belonged to the larger U.S. society, whose ethos challenged the norms and expectations of this Arab Muslim community. In public school especially, Yemeni Americans faced a different model for success in life than the one they knew in their home culture. Historically, U.S. education has tended toward a republican ideal, which emerged from Western Europe. The classic republican model includes the separation of church and state; the importance of the individual; the central role of rational and political factors rather than cultural and sociogeographic factors in the construction of citizenship; and the unifying function assigned to state institutions, particularly to the school, in building the reproduction of these values (Van Zanten 1997). Layla's case and excerpts from the other Yemeni girls' lives illustrate that an inevitable clash occurs at the intersection of U.S. republican values and the sociocultural practices of the Southend, where the Yemeni community lived by the following: an emphasis on ritual and religious practice, the prominence of the family, the focal role of cultural and sociogeopolitical factors relating Yemen in the construction of ethnic identity, and kinship relations through the father's line or "village" in constructing the reproduction of these characteristics. The *hijabat*, who, on the one hand, attempted to be individuals in their own right and, on the other hand, complied with their community's expectations, experienced an intellectual, if not emotional, divide as they traveled in and out of their homes in the Southend.

The girls maintained dual identities, which bifurcated according to the gendered, economic, and cultural spaces they inhabited. Although this mingling of spaces made school more social and liberating for the girls, it posed a danger to their clearly demarcated home and community spaces. At this juncture, they were forced to imagine Yemen as their homeland and all that it entailed in their daily lives in the Southend and at school.

It could be argued that Layla and her friends were powerless, at least much more so than most typical high school students, but this would be a rather simplistic observation because, after all, these students were successfully maintaining cultural norms both at home and at school. As Gibson (1997) observes, minority populations do well in school when they are strongly supported by their families. This was the case for the *hijabat*, even though their parents typically came from low socioeconomic backgrounds and had either very little or no formal schooling. Nevertheless, the girls were surrounded by family who were protective and supportive of their high school education, and, in a few cases, of a possible college education. It may turn out that this strong support and family identification will be the mechanism by which the girls will achieve their goals, if not immediately after high school graduation, then perhaps a few years later, once they have married and had a child or two—depending on their spouses' disposition toward education. One of the girls' fathers, for example, negotiated for his daughter, as part of the marriage agreement in Yemen, that her husband would allow her to continue her education should she want to do so.

At least for this first generation of Yemeni Americans, the sojourner identification was strong and relevant. Home constituted a set of relationships among people both in the Southend and in Yemen. For girls like Layla, Yemen and its cultural and religious values were ever present in their lives, even when they had never traveled there. However, the *hijabat* were sojourners who did not completely identify with the United States or Yemen as their home, but instead found a "home" in managing their liminal space. As settlers who not only dreamed of returning home but actually made the sojourn home, the Yemeni families of the Southend gave credence to the idea that the physical and the imagined space are at times one and the same.

Chapter 3
Classroom as Oasis

In class it's different. We talk to each other.

Webster's New World Dictionary defines *oasis* as "any place or thing offering welcome relief as from difficulty or dullness." Unlike the hallways or cafeteria at Cobb High, the classroom offered the Yemeni American students, boys and girls alike, a sanctuary from social and cultural norms, a place unlike any other space. Within the school setting, and foremost among the girls' dispositions toward school and social life, was their worry of perception—how they were perceived by others. Research on adolescence and especially on girls (see Brown and Gilligan 1992; Finders 1997; Thorne 1997) suggests that this is typical of adolescent development more generally. Teenagers' preoccupation with how their peers view them is indeed a characteristic of youth culture and, as popular media would indicate, an all-consuming one. However, in the case of girls such as Layla or her good friend Aisha, the self-other anxiety was directed toward specific people, that is, Yemeni boys as the primary constant and Yemeni girls as a secondary but important indicator of acceptance or rejection. The classroom provided an alternative way of being, or what Greene (1997) calls an "alternative reality," for the *hijabat* because it was considered a private space and was not made part of the public practice of gossip, which pervaded the halls and cafeteria. In fact, unlike Finder's (1997) study on thirteen-year-olds, in which she found that the classroom as safe haven is a myth and therefore unsafe, especially for girls who were not "social queens," I found the classroom to be the only space within Cobb High where boys and girls interacted socially as they would in any public school. In other words, what constitutes "unsafe" or "uncomfortable" in one setting, as in Finder's study, may be liberating in the Yemeni American context.

The lives of the Yemeni American girls were clearly demarcated by physical boundaries that impacted their social and academic lives. In the previous chapter, the notion of sojourner illustrates the complex spatial relationships that permeated the girls' quotidian lives. In Cobb High School, the complexity exhibited by the interaction of Yemeni immigrants, Yemeni Americans, and non–Arab Americans only reiterated the importance of understanding that politics of space are made all the more complex by language, dress, ethnicity, gender, and social class. As Jackson (1968/1990) observed in his study of classrooms, "*Behind the ordinary lies the extraordinary*" (xix). In other words, the study of classroom life uncovers much and for girls such as Layla, classroom life was really an oasis.

One way to think about the classroom setting is to organize the events that take place there and those that take place in the halls or cafeteria within Goffman's (1959) framework of interaction versus performance. According to Goffman, interaction is defined as the "reciprocal influence of individuals upon one another's actions when in one another's immediate presence" (15). Performance as he defined it encompasses all of a participant's activity on a given occasion that serves to influence in any way any of the other participants. The performance is preestablished; it is a routine of sorts from which social relationships arise. For example, in one classroom in which I observed Yemeni boys and girls conversing easily with one another in both English and Arabic, one of the boys informed me, when I inquired about the boys' lack of conversation in the cafeteria, that if someone (of Arab/Yemeni background) were to come in and see the students sitting as a group, this boy would be questioned about his actions, especially if he were seen talking to Saba. Saba agreed to this but added that she, as a girl, and not he, would suffer the consequences. He continued to say that the lunchroom really showed the way things were (whereas the classroom is the anomaly)—the boys "hang out with the clan [in the cafeteria] and that this is nature and natural." This example shows that neither the boys nor the girls were concerned about anyone seeing them chat along with other classmates during class. It was unlikely that a parent, community member, or other Yemeni students would enter the class and observe the interaction among the students. The classroom was a safe zone, an oasis—it was not easily entered or exited. Furthermore, and as Goffman's framework suggests, whereas the lunchroom and cafeteria gave rise to the "enactment of rights and duties attached to a given status," (16) which the performer routinely reenacts for the same audience, the classroom invited varieties of face-to-face interaction, especially among girls. In the classroom, as many of the teachers pointed out, the girls were at their best academically and often much more social than in any of the other school settings.[1] Hallways and the cafeteria were places where behavior was sanctioned by cultural and religious practices and where power, as was

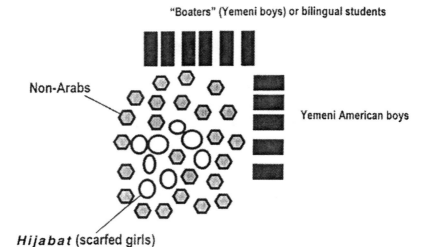

Figure 1. Cafeteria

explained in Chapter 2, was exerted to a full extent by the male gaze in much the same way that it was in the streets of the Southend or in a village in Yemen. In effect, the boys' gaze was location bound, with the classroom as a blind spot (to the panopticon's power). The classroom became the place where the boys' vision and the *hijabat*'s perception of their gaze were altered.

The Cafeteria

The *hijabat* placed a high value on school life, high enough to perform according to their community's norms both socially and academically. Continuing their high school education meant being fully conscious of themselves as Yemenis in the cafeteria and hallways. Therefore, the girls and boys did not sit near each other and did not talk to or look at one another. This reflected cultural norms both in the Southend and in Yemen, where men and women usually dined in separate rooms in restaurants. The *hijabat* at Cobb High sat at tables that were in a small cluster in the middle of the cafeteria. This cluster was buffered by tables at which non-Arab boys and/or girls or Arabs (Palestinians, Iraqis, or Lebanese) sat. The Yemeni American boys sat far away on one side of the room in a row of tables, while the newly arrived Yemeni boys ("boaters"), who made up the majority of the bilingual program, sat on the adjacent side of the room. Figure 1 illustrates a typical lunch hour in the cafeteria. The Yemeni boys who were part of the bilingual program were especially watchful of the *hijabat*, and both boys and girls took notice when the two sexes drew near each other. Sometimes the Yemeni boys reacted negatively toward girls or women they did not know. An example of this occurred near the end of my second year of fieldwork as I pre- pared to shadow Aisha from class to class throughout the day. Aisha approached me furtively on the day I was to shadow her and said, "I have to tell you something. There's this guy. He's my cousin. He saw me talking to you at lunch yesterday and he asked me why you were talking to me. He went to my house after school yesterday and told my mother that I should not talk to you, or my reputation will be ruined. So, can you please not shadow me today?" Of course, I agreed, but I reminded her that I had her mother's consent to shadow her. She said, "I know. He's been saying things to me since last year. But now, he went to my mother. I'm really sorry. I'm so embarrassed. No one knows about this. None of my friends. You won't tell them?" I reassured her that I would not, but I asked if I could still sit at her table during lunch because other girls in the study would be there. She responded, "That's just it. He isn't in that lunch period, but yesterday he was. But you can eat with us. You know Layla and those guys." Aisha seemed frightened during the entire conversation. She feared her cousin, who was younger than she was. At the time I was awed by the power her tenth grade cousin exerted over her and, inadvertently, over me. In the cafeteria, the girls kept their eyes away from the sides of the room, while the boys stayed away from the cluster of *hijabat*. Only brothers or close cousins conversed with the girls, and sometimes husbands talked to their wives, but this usually occurred in the halls and not in the cafeteria.

The girls explained their behavior in the cafeteria in one of two ways: shame or fear. Saba, who was more religiously minded than the other girls and who could quote the Qur'an at length, asserted, "Shame and not fear [was] what the girls feel around boys." In the Qur'an, she argued among her friends, it was stated that girls should be modest and must act so in public places, such as the cafeteria. Consequently, most of the girls not only shied away from the Yemeni boys during lunch but also all other young men, including the teachers. It was rare to see one of the *hijabat* waving to a male teacher or principal or even saying hello as other non-Arab girls did. In addition, the *hijabat* rarely sat with stu- dents unlike themselves. For example, an aerial view of the cafeteria would show white or black scarfed heads in small circles, all leaning towards the center of the table, much like closed flower blooms. When a nonscarfed girl sat among the *hijabat*, it was immediately noticed and noticeable. Consequently, when a girl wore the *hijab* and then decided not to wear it, she was cast out of the *hijabat* group and was usually no longer welcome by most of the girls. This occurred to Hannah, a Moroccan girl who had worn the scarf for two months at her friends' urging, but found it alien to her, especially because she had never worn one in Morocco. Hannah complained that the Yemeni girls no longer talked to her and thought her shameless. She made friends elsewhere, among the nonscarfed Lebanese and non-Arab girls.

Shame was a powerful incentive for proper behavior or performance in the cafeteria, because as the girls explained, it was grounded in Yemeni culture and religion. In public places, unlike the classroom, all the *hijabat* were modest in their mannerisms, movement, and speech. They kept to themselves within a specific area of the cafeteria. The only exception to this performance occurred when there were fights between Arabs and non-Arabs. For example, when a non-Arab boy threw food at one of the *hijabat*, the Yemeni boys hurried to protect the *hijabat* by fighting with the non-Arab boys. Exhibiting shame or modesty, then, was a public performance, one that was demanded by Yemeni culture (and expected by the boys) and enacted by the girls. But, why and how was this behavior sustained over time? What mechanism reinforced the cultural enactment of shame when the *hijabat* were also part of American social norms in the cafeteria?

While shame was a publicly enacted performance to be seen again and again in the cafeteria and other public places, fear of being found without "shame" prompted the girls' public performances. The *hijabat* often acted out of fear. Amani, one of the *hijabat* with aspirations to become a nurse pointed out, "They'll [the guys] just talk about you. They'll like ruin your rep. Like for us, the most, like, well, not the most important thing but we have to like, you know, watch our reputations really, really careful." Fear of gossip prompted the *hijabat* to perform according to what was expected of them. In fact, they were quite supportive of one another in that endeavor, both in the hallways and in the cafeteria. Even when one of the *hijabat* was quite alone in the hallway or the cafeteria, she was very conservative in her behavior. Goffman (1959) has remarked that "when a performer guides his private activity in accordance with incorporated moral standards, he may associate these standards with a reference group of some kind, thus creating a non-present audience for his activity" (81). The *hijabat* automatically assumed a different role when they were in the cafeteria and did so as a group, differing significantly from a clique. Again, Goffman is useful here because he links performance to the notion of team. In the case of the *hijabat*, they were first and foremost members of a team through their dress and, importantly, their scarves. In addition, a teammate "is someone whose dramaturgical co-operation one is dependent upon in fostering a given definition of the situation. . . . Similarly, a girl at a party who is flagrantly accessible may be shunned by the other girls who are present, but in certain matters she is part of their team and cannot fail to threaten the definition they are collectively maintaining that girls are difficult sexual prizes (Goffman 1959:83). In effect, the *hijabat's* fear of gossip was rooted in how they were perceived as sexual entities. They all denied that possibility. During lunch they ate with one another and never faced outward, only inward within their cluster of tables. They collectively formed a private sphere that was difficult to enter or exit without the *hijab*.

The Hallways

The hallways of Cobb High School posed a challenge for the *hijabat*. Hallways, by definition, are places of movement, both fast and slow. And not all hallways are the same. For instance, hallways can become congested as was often the case in B Hall, or, as the *hijabat* would often say, the "Boater Hall." This hall was usually congested by the recent Yemeni arrivals simply because all of their social studies classrooms were located in this hall. The *hijabat* were especially careful in this hall, where they usually lowered their eyes, walked quickly but not too fast, avoided body contact, and kept quiet. Just as in the cafeteria, the girls feared the new arrivals much more than the American-born boys of Yemeni descent. The so-called boaters were the ones who reported back to families in the Southend. For example, the following observations illustrate the very real perceived threat the *hijabat* experienced on a daily basis:

> After lunch, Saba and I walk down the hallway. She tells me about "this guy, Jeff. He saw me and said, 'Saba, you look nice today.' He tried to put his arm around my shoulders, but I moved away and he said that my shoulders got wider. I just stepped away before he touched me. But, then, there was this boater and he looked at me when this happened. But I don't think he knows who I am. I won't wear this outfit [purple *abaya* and scarf] for two months."
> Several days later, Saba sees the same Yemeni boy again in the gym class in which she is one of the student leaders. She tells me that the boater who saw her is in the class and he *looked* at her. Now, he knows who she is. I ask her whether it's the new Yemeni boys or all of the Yemeni boys who threaten the girls with "telling." She says that it's the boaters usually. "They feel it's their duty. The ones who are born here, a few do, but most don't."

As a Muslim girl, Saba could not be seen interacting at any level with a non-Muslim boy by a Yemeni Muslim boy. The fact that the boater gave her a "look" meant to Saba that he noticed the interaction and blamed her for Jeff's behavior even though she was the recipient and not the instigator of Jeff's compliment. She moved away because she could not be touched by a man who is not her father, brother, uncle, or very close cousin. Yet, although Saba behaved appropriately, the Yemeni boy witnessed the scene and was likely to remember her and find out her name later if he noticed her again. In the meantime, Saba, who did not want to be noticed, decided not to wear the same *abaya* and scarf for a long time. She did not want to provoke this Yemeni boy to speak against her to her family. Secretly, Saba told me that she was pleased by Jeff's compliment but had the presence of mind to perform according to cultural norms, yet her fear was very real and escalated when she found out that the boater was in her gym class.

Although the *hijabat* were watchful in the hallways, they were less likely to maintain the cluster group from the cafeteria all the time. In the hallways, some of the girls walked and talked with their non-Arab friends and other *hijabat*; they tended to be louder and to joke more. They had a favorite bathroom in A Hall, in which they stopped to rearrange their scarves, gossip, and snack. This bathroom was generally full of cigarette smoke, although the girls swore that they never smoked because it is forbidden in the Qur'an. This was puzzling because it was never clear who was smoking in there. In general, then, hallway life was less constrained than that of the cafeteria, but from this emerged a different type of watchfulness—the girls watched one another more, in much the same way that Goffman (1959) describes the promiscuous girl at a party being watched by other girls in case she goes too far and hurts the team. Nadya, who was a ninth grader during my first year of fieldwork, was especially watchful of other girls' behavior in the halls. New to Cobb High, Nadya worried about being proper in the hallways and cafeteria, even though she was quite boisterous in class. During one of the times I shadowed Nadya, I observed the following: "We leave English. In the hallway, we see one of the *hijabat* giving an exuberant hug to a girl with long blond hair who is not Arab. Both girls laugh hard and loudly. Nadya comments, 'Some of the Arab girls in this school, I don't like. They're all messed up. They do stuff with boys, bad stuff, like talk to them, go out with them.'" Nadya's comment was telling. Being loud and laughter were associated with overt behavior that then indexed inappropriate behavior with boys. Nadya did not know either of the girls she observed, yet the exuberance they exhibited indicated to her that the Arab girl was "all messed up" and that she probably "does stuff with boys." The implications Nadya drew from her observations seem unreasonable, yet they reflected the teachings of the Arabic school she attended and perhaps her own family's admonitions about overt behavior. She was also struggling to fit into her new school and to understand the cultural limitations, both American and Yemeni, which she faced in different contexts. The following example illustrates that although the hallways may have been less constraining because movement was categorically manifested, there was still a certain degree of watchfulness

among the girls, and this reminded Nadya that an adequate performance regardless of audience was still important: "As we walk, we see a
girl who covers her face, except for the eyes. She notices that Nadya's
scarf isn't covering her completely and that some skin just below the
neck is showing. She exclaims rather loudly, 'Haram!' and points an
index finger at the spot of skin that is showing. Nadya hurries to cover
herself, before anyone sees. I notice that Nadya seems rather anxious
that her scarf wasn't just right. She tugs at it surreptitiously throughout
the day."

The loud exclamation in Arabic for *forbidden* by the girl who noticed
the spot of skin would normally have been thought of as too loud, but
in this instance, because it called attention to the personal appearance
of a fellow *hijabat*, the loudness was not even noticed. Nadya was grateful
that she could repair the damage before anyone else noticed the uncovered spot that could harm her reputation.

The hallways of Cobb High, like all hallways in various high schools,
were lively and loud. The students were usually rushing to get to their
next class on time and paid little attention to the people into whom they
bumped or to the laughter they heard. Among the *hijabat*, however, hallway life was different. Although they did meet friends at their lockers
and walked together to class, they maintained a distance from the
goings-on of their nonscarfed peers. They did not take part of the same
play, and their performance was meant to be witnessed by an audience
that was likely to approve of them as modest and good girls. This alone
made the hallway an important social context for the girls. In the following section, I discuss how the classroom itself was perhaps the most liberating of all social and academic environments in the high school.

Classroom as Oasis

The classroom, regardless of subject matter, was the only space within
the high school in which Yemeni American boys and girls talked to one
another. Teachers observed that the girls were quieter than the boys and
sat apart from them, but there was much more interaction among them
than in any other space. The *hijabat* were more likely to speak freely to
the American-born Yemeni and would ignore the boys who were part of
the bilingual program.[2] The *hijabat* also interacted more with the non-
Arabs in the class. The teachers sometimes enforced mixed seating (and
more will be said about this in Chapter 4), which decreased the level of
talk and interaction in class, but when this was not the case, interaction
among the students followed two distinctive phases, each of which is
made up of two possible scenarios.

Figure 2 shows that the students arranged themselves in one of two

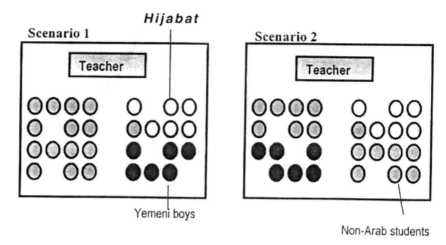

Figure 2. Classroom Phase 1

ways when they first arrived in class. Scenario 1 was the more likely scenario, where both the *hijabat* and the Yemeni American boys sat on one side of the room and the non-Arabs sat on the other. Scenario 2 is the case in which the *hijabat* sat on one side of the room and the Yemeni boys sat on the other, while the non-Arab students sat on both sides. In both scenarios the *hijabat* and the Yemeni American boys sat as two distinct groups, without mixing with one another or the non-Arab students. The non-Arab students were either organized by gender or were mixed, but they all talked to one another. While these spatial arrangements may seem to extend, at first glance, cafeteria cultural norms into the classroom, this was not so. Once the teacher took attendance and the lesson began, whether it was a lecture, film, individual seatwork, or group work, the students moved in astonishing ways, which would be impossible outside the room. Moving was voluntary among students and usually occurred once the teacher assigned a task. For example, Figure 3 shows phase 2, an interactive setting where gender, ethnicity, and language (Arabic and English) mixed together in what most teachers and students would recognize as a typical American classroom full of adolescents.

In general, the *hijabat* were more comfortable in the classroom than elsewhere in the school. Unlike Finder's (1997) study, in which she found that only girls who have popular power feel most comfortable in class, that was not the case among the *hijabat*. The *hijabat*, who normally kept to themselves in all public places, were unusually interactive in the

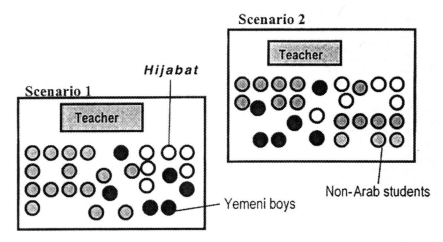

Figure 3. Classroom Phase 2

classroom. The boys were also more open with the *hijabat* and the non-Arab students. The following excerpt from my field notes is an example of the social interaction that usually occurred in the classroom.

> On one side of the room sit all the Arab girls. Layla was moved by the teacher across the room because she talked too much to Sumayya. Once Mr. Fallstein begins his lecture, she moves back next to Sumayya and Aisha. One of the *hijabat* sits by herself in the corner. There are eight girls with scarves. Two Arab boys are absent because they're at the mosque. One Arab boy sits by himself in a corner. Sumayya tells me that she doubts that these two are really at the mosque praying. She then talks to a non-Arab boy next to her about homework. He wants to borrow her homework.
> In the meantime, Mr. Fallstein covers senators' and representatives' qualifications for the job and writes these on the blackboard. He has his back to the class and talks over the conversations in the room. Layla gets teased by a boy who is across the room from her and talks to another non-Arab boy and non-Arab girl near her. The boy across the room asks if he can sit next to her. The non-Arab boy comes to sit by Layla and says hi to me. He teases her and Sumayyah by asking them out to a Rave and on dates. They giggle and tease back, saying that they'll meet him on Friday night at the party. They're both embarrassed that I'm listening. Layla and Sumayya tell me in the hall later that they're just friends with him and they always talk to these boys in class.

The question one must ask, then, is why was the classroom such a unique space for the Yemeni American students? How did they reconcile two such distinct ways of being within the school building walls? One salient way to distinguish the classroom from other high school spaces is to understand that the classroom did not require the normative performance of other public spaces, the enactment of codified roles by either the *hijabat* or their male counterparts. Their identities became those of American students rather than Yemeni ones. In the classroom, interaction among the students was often spontaneous; thus normative gender relations tended to be of lesser import during subject matter activities. Furthermore, there was an adult, the teacher, such as Mr. Fallstein, who sanctioned acceptable and unacceptable behavior, and the students did not necessarily have to be responsible for themselves when they had a teacher who set classroom policy for interactive engagement. Also and in general, the teachers at Cobb High lectured or used recitation strategies or what Cazden (1988) calls three-part sequence questions that include teacher initiation, student response, and teacher evaluation. Asking students a question and then responding by saying "right" or "wrong" was most common. There was very little sustained discussion in the classrooms I observed, and once the teachers assigned a task students did individual seatwork. This type of academic interaction actually fostered more social discourse. Real-world cultural norms were suspended in the classroom for the Yemeni American students, and other types of norms took over, ones that were common to most high school classrooms. Yet how did the *hijabat* and Yemeni American boys make sense of their own discourse in and out of the classroom? One would expect that inner conflict over proper behavior and the maintenance of "good girl" status would ensue. However, this was not the case.

"In class it's different. We talk to each other," Aisha said. As Aisha's comment suggests, the classroom was different, and there were three common arguments the *hijabat* gave for their contrary behavior in the classroom versus that of the hallways and the cafeteria. First, there was the "we know each other; it's like talking to a brother or cousin" argument. The girls pointed out that they had known the boys with whom they spoke in the classroom since they were small children in the neighborhood, and therefore these boys seemed much like family. Second, there was the "it's safe—no one talks" argument. The *hijabat* thought of the classroom as a haven from prying eyes and gossip. And, interestingly enough, the goings-on of the classroom, even those that included teasing among boys and girls as in the previous example, remained in the room. One teacher noted that when she had only girls in her class, she would lock the classroom door and they sometimes removed their scarves to be more comfortable, something that would never occur anywhere else outside their homes unless they were among women at a party or wedding. Third, there was the "we're just talking about school stuff and there's nothing wrong with that" argument given by the *hija-*

bat. This argument was used often by the girls when they explained themselves to a person of authority, such as a teacher or family member.

All three arguments utilized by the *hijabat* helped them negotiate two different worlds and make an oasis of the classroom. By temporarily giving the boys in the classroom the status of family member, they bridged the gap between home and school to make life at school more "normal" and home life less threatening. The fact that the girls felt safe from gossip encouraged them to engage more openly both in academic talk—that is, talk around school work—and social talk—talk about social events and relationships. Their openness, however, was predicated by the reciprocity of the Yemeni boys in the class. Their comfort level decreased as the number of boaters increased. They were much more comfortable with Yemeni American boys than with the newly arrived immigrants. In fact, when the girls found themselves in a classroom with mostly boaters, they were less likely to move around the room and chat with friends, but they were still more interactive than in the halls or the cafeteria. For their part, and with few exceptions, the recent immigrant boys kept to themselves. I should note again that I often observed when one of the *hijabat* found herself as the sole wearer of the *hijab* in a classroom, she was likely to drop the class and find one in which she was certain there would be others who wore the *hijab*. This occurred among a few of the older girls, who found themselves alone in the more advanced math, economics, or science classes. These girls were generally good students, whose friends sometimes dropped out of school or did not see the point of taking the "hard" classes when they knew that they would not continue their education after high school. Although the *hijabat* were always wary of the boys' watchful gazes, for the most part, the classroom still offered a safe zone, an oasis.

It is important to consider why the boys might have felt freer to speak to the girls in the classroom. They too gave similar arguments as those of the girls. The classroom was less constraining, and the presence of the teacher, a third party, as was commonly said by both boys and girls, "keeps the devil away." In addition, some of the Yemeni American and recent immigrant boys were engaged to be married or were married.[3] Therefore talking to the girls was not a "sin" because they said they could control themselves, that is, "their lust," in their married status. For instance, one eighteen-year-old Yemeni American boy who had two children and was married at fifteen to a girl from Yemen said, "If I didn't get married, I'd be lost. Marriage controls hormones. That's what my father says. Life is different here. We have a house and my mother helps with the children." A friend of his who was sitting next to me and Nouria, the girl I was shadowing that day, added, "I'm going to Yemen this summer and marry a girl there. It's too hard to get married in the

U.S. If I didn't marry, I'd be lost and start drinking, smoking. Marriage fixes everything." At least for some boys, another argument to be made for the more open classroom interaction was that they were already married, and therefore the talk was innocent. For the *hijabat,* the classroom was a space that counted tremendously in their daily lives. It was the only space in which the girls openly interacted with people unlike themselves, as in Mr. Fallstein's classroom. To an outside observer the classroom became an extraordinary setting, one that defied the performative norms that defined all other spaces in the high school. The classroom could be characterized as a space of mutual social engagement and interaction that was spontaneous, whereas the cafeteria and halls called for a performance for a very strict and threatening audience, whether real or imagined. It was no wonder that the *hijabat* looked forward to school with both anticipation and trepidation. The girls often felt that home life in general, and especially during summer vacations, was boring for them because social and spatial relationships were limited to family and close family friends within the Southend, whereas school offered more, and the classroom offered even more in relative safety.

Chapter 4

Islam and Conflicting Visions of Literacy

Saba and I went shopping at the mall. She wanted to buy gifts for her friends and family for the El Eid holiday. I parked the car in the lot in front of JC Penney and moved to open my door. Saba raised her hand without saying anything and I stopped moving. She closed her eyes and her mouth began to move silently. I surreptitiously glanced at my watch and saw that it was nearly noon. Saba was doing her noon prayer right in the front passenger seat, while I sat there not knowing what to do. I caught a few sounds, but her lips moved silently for ten minutes. When she finished, Saba praised God aloud, took off her seatbelt, and unlocked the door.

"In-betweenness" describes the textual space in which youth, in this case, Yemeni American girls—the *hijabat*—made sense of their lives as high school students and good Muslim daughters, sisters, and mothers. They employed religious, secular, and Arabic texts as a means for negotiating home and school worlds. As I mentioned earlier, home and school worlds mean the various institutional, cultural, familial, and linguistic relationships these girls had in spaces that are normatively construed as home and school. Home and school spaces often overlapped one another and were inherently related, therefore the boundaries between them shifted constantly as the girls negotiated social, academic, and cultural norms.

The girls' use of text and literacy became integral to their social and academic success. Here, I offer a view of literacy that is conceptualized from a sociocultural, sociolinguistic, and ethnographic perspective to illustrate the importance of the in-between texts with which the *hijabat* constructed gender, ethnic, socioeconomic, and religious identities that allowed them access to taboo topics and/or mainstream American cultural practices. The girls' textual practices had a powerful impact on their participation in school. I also use the term "in-between" because the girls often used it to describe themselves. For example, when Aisha, an incredibly motivated and bright student, described herself to me and explained that she did not meet her mother's expectations of being a good daughter, she shook her head and said, "In-between. Not what she'd want me to be, you know." Her mother preferred that Aisha be more Yemeni and less American.

Framing and Theorizing In-betweenness

Within the larger frame of research on youth, the notion of in-between-ness contributes to a body of research that has in recent years placed greater emphasis on adolescent literacy practices outside of school and the notion of existence in multiple worlds (Alvermann, Hinchman, Moore, Phelps, and Waff 1998; Moje 2000). Defined as such, the notion of in-betweenness and in-between texts can be characterized as a power-ful heuristic that adds important insight to our understanding of literacy and discourse. The *hijabat* used secular and religious texts to negotiate appropriate social and academic spaces for themselves in and out of school, and the notion of in-betweenness distinguishes these texts from other ways of being. The texts that the girls used can be described as in-between texts because they are forms of discourse that were manifested in different contexts and that bridge, subvert, and re-create Yemeni and American social and cultural norms.

By discourse, I mean more than talk or speech acts.[1] For example, Gee (1989) distinguishes discourse (stretches of language) from Discourse: "ways of being in the world; they are forms of life which integrate words, acts, values, beliefs, attitudes, and social identities as well as gestures, glances, body positions, and clothes" (6). Gee (1996) asserts further that a Discourse is an "identity kit" that a person takes on as a role and that is immediately recognizable to others (7). In the tradition of Goff-man (1959), who argues that participants' actions, talk, and perform-ances are intimately connected and related to those with whom they share the interaction, Gee suggests that Discourse is really a presenta-tion of the self, both past and present. Both Goffman (1981) and Davies and Harré (1990) associate the presentation of self and identity as rela-tional activities whose textual performance is mediated by the space that participants occupy. However, whereas Davies and Harré argue that par-ticipants' positioning is guided by their own autobiographical percep-tions, Goffman's view suggests that positioning, or in his words, footing, is a relational conceptualization of interaction rather than a state of mind. By its very nature, relational conceptualization presupposes a pri-ori experience as well as the present, coconstructed experience of inter-action. Goffman (1959) noted that "when an individual appears before others his actions will influence the definition of the situation which they come to have" (6). Goffman adds that sometimes individuals will intentionally express themselves according to the traditions of the group to which they belong in order to create a favorable or necessary impression. In a very real sense, Goffman's notion of interaction is connected to Gee's definition of Discourse in that both describe culture and participants' related textual practices.

According to Geertz (1973), culture "denotes an historically transmitted pattern of meanings embodied in symbols, a system of inherited conceptions expressed in symbolic forms by means of which men communicate, perpetuate, and develop their knowledge about attitudes toward life" (89). Hence culture is both a temporal and a local phenomenon. It is certainly not static because the enactment of Discourse or culture as performance is localized continuously over time and is therefore dynamic. The locus of such a performance can be an individual or group of individuals who assume culturally laden roles that require certain texts, behaviors, mannerisms, and so on. The example of Saba (a twelfth grader), whose experience I chose as a symbolic entrée into this chapter, illustrates that she, as a devout Muslim, is closely following the strictures governing the five pillars of Islam—one of which is prayer five times daily.[2] At the same time, her oral text is mediated by the space she occupies and creates something that is representative of both her surroundings and her culture. Saba's discourse can be described as in-between and her performance is symbolic of adaptation to her immediate context. The cultural pattern is explicit yet somewhat changed to account for difference, both in identity and in space. She bridged and re-created her American and Yemeni identities in the car.

This frame of reference—in-betweenness—is especially helpful in delineating the contextual uses of texts and language among the Yemeni American students. For example, the use of Arabic in school served important functional and religious purposes as students attempted to maintain dual identities. It is not clear, however, whether cultural differences in communication style between home and school have a direct cause-and-effect relationship on school achievement (Erickson 1987). While in the field, I observed that communication style is important in making social adjustments within the school setting and, in particular, in the classroom, but not necessarily in academic performance. For these students, social success in school (behaving and communicating appropriately according to cultural and religious traditions) was as important as academic achievement because the enactment of appropriate social mores in and out of school determined status as well as degrees of shame and honor.

The localization of Saba's prayer was unexpected, at least to me, as we sat in the mall parking lot, yet her actions symbolized an identification with something other than the tangible objects in the immediate space of the car. Under the usual circumstances, Saba would have found a quiet area at home or at the mosque, washed her hands and feet, laid out a small rug, and knelt facing east on her knees for her prayer. Instead, she improvised as best she could and made use of the car, which was facing east toward Mecca, and prayed silently in Arabic. This improvisation, a performance, identified Saba solidly with a people and a religion. As Goffman (1959) might note, Saba wanted to create the right impression during this interaction even though I am not a Yemeni or Muslim member of her community. Her actions, which were both textual and spiritual, transcended her immediate space and occupied an in-between space that was neither Yemeni nor American but was instead a hybrid, an alternative possibility carved out of a particular time (afternoon) and place (the car outside the mall). Bhabha (1994), who has written extensively on culture in the post–colonial era and about the boundary spaces that minority populations occupy, characterizes this in-betweenness as the locality of culture. He argues that locality is "more . . . hybrid in the articulation of cultural differences and identifications than can be represented in any hierarchical or binary structuring of social antagonism" (140). In other words, in-betweenness, or the locality of culture, signifies the immediate adaptation of one's performance or identity to one's textual, social, cultural, and physical surroundings. Saba engaged in ritualistic performances that were influenced by the immediate conditions of the interaction. In effect, the result was neither conventionally Yemeni/Muslim nor commonly American but somewhere in between. Insofar as literacy is concerned, and as the title of the chapter implies, visions of literacy did conflict with one another because the girls occupied the in-between spaces of two cultures and this necessitated negotiation, which in turn influenced ritual performance as they engaged with texts (reading, writing, and oracy).

One way to frame the analysis that follows is to use Scribner's (1984) definition of literacy as three metaphors—literacy as adaptation, literacy as power, and literacy as a state of grace. This is apropos in the case of the Yemeni American girls because their discourse reflected their attempts to adapt to both American and Yemeni norms, to achieve power in being print literate in both Arabic and English, and to be full of grace through reading and embodying religious text. Ethnographic research relies on the description of a cultural site in a given moment and an analysis of "Ah ha!" moments during that time (Willis and Trondman, 2000), and these textual moments in which the *hijabat* engaged with text provide unique "Ah has" into their Yemeni and American worlds. Scribner argues, "Literacy has neither a static nor a universal essence" (8). In describing the Muslim Vai people of West Africa, Scribner and her colleagues attributed various literacy practices to cultural competencies required in different contexts. Literacy as adaptation, for instance, "is designed to capture concepts of literacy that emphasize its survival or pragmatic value" (9). Literacy as power, according to Scribner, focuses on the relationship between group mobilization and literacy. The third metaphor, literacy as a state of grace, emphasizes the notion that the literate person is endowed with special virtues. Scribner notes, for example, that "memorizing the *Qur'an*—literally taking its words into you and making them part of yourself—is simultaneously a process of becoming both literate and holy" (13). I use these metaphors as I describe the girls' uses of text in several places and how in-betweenness was manifested at school, weddings and parties, Arabic school, and Muhathara (lecture).

Hidden Texts in School

Scribner notes that the "the single most compelling fact about literacy is that it is a social achievement" and, importantly, that "literacy is the outcome of cultural transmission" (1984:7). Among the Yemeni students in the Southend, being literate meant being able to call upon multiple literacies in order to perform appropriately in the contexts they inhabited. School, for example, may have created an imbalance in the lives of Yemeni American students by challenging their cultural traditions and by challenging their primary (or home) Discourse (Gee 1989). Whereas the Muslim Yemeni family promotes loyalty based on kinship ties, U.S. schools tend to privilege individual opportunity over collective responsibility. American schools teach youngsters to value personal response, individual reasoning, and the expression of a highly personal voice (Graff 1995; Portes and Rumbaut 1996). An example of this is found in the Michigan English and Language Arts Framework standards for public schools. In these standards, students are strongly encouraged to form an individual voice so that they can question texts and form arguments about them, thus often disregarding their own beliefs or values about the content and ways to talk or write about it. Home or family culture is necessarily divorced from the students' learning at school in order for knowledge to be disseminated most efficiently. This type of critical reading of texts, when it does take place and that Gee (1989) calls "a liberating metaknowledge or literacy," carries an ideological message that may run counter to Yemeni Muslims' views about the sanctity of religious text (i.e., the Qur'an) in relation to their quotidian Discourses both at home and at school. (It is important to note that Anyon [1981] argues that the critical analysis of texts in the classroom is rare and is influenced by social class practices. Her research shows that knowledge is often fragmented and isolated from meaning.) Knowing how to read at school is different from knowing how to read at home, where the Qur'an is the primary source of reading. Reading the Qur'an and being able to recite it endows a person with both knowledge and holiness, or, in Scribner's words, a state of grace. In fact, in the Qur'an itself, there is a passage that states, "This is a perfect book. There is no doubt in it," which makes it impossible for students to be critical of the word of God. Both Yemeni boys and girls at Cobb High School told me that all I needed to do was to read the Qur'an in order to know what success is. In other words and according to them, the text of the Qur'an contains all, and if one reads it, that person assumes that same knowledge.

The literacy practices with which the *hijabat* engaged were clearly influenced by their religion. Street (1995) defines literacy practices as "behaviour and the social and cultural conceptualizations that give meaning to the uses of reading and/or writing" (2). They incorporate literacy events, which refer to how a piece of writing is integral to a reader's or writer's interaction or interpretation of it (Heath 1982). Street's definition of literacy practices is part of a larger framework stemming from various disciplines called New Literacy Studies. According to Gee (1999b):

> The New Literacy Studies approach literacy as part and parcel of, and inextricable from, specific social, cultural, institutional, and political practices. Thus literacy is, in a sense, "multiple": literacy becomes different "literacies," as reading and writing are differently and distinctively shaped and transformed inside different sociocultural practices. Additionally, these sociocultural practices always have inherent and value-laden, but often different, implications about what count as "acceptable" identities, actions, and ways of knowing. They are, in this sense, deeply "political." (356)

In other words, as Barton and Hamilton (1998) have pointed out, literacy is integral to its context. At school, where the intersection of multiple cultures and literacies was most evident, Yemeni American girls learned to adapt various texts to different situations. The most direct way that they did this was by organizing some behaviors and speech events into three categories that stem from the Qur'an and religious teachings. The three categories were *haram*, meaning forbidden; *halal*, meaning lawful; and *mahkru*, meaning not written as forbidden in the Qur'an but condemned by the Prophet Muhammad. All things *haram* are written in the Qur'an. Drinking alcohol, for example, is *haram*. Things *halal* are good deeds, which include learning and being learned. Things *mahkru* include wearing makeup before marriage or listening to music. The *mahkru* category is controversial and is therefore the marked category. Many of the *hijabat* wore nail polish or eyeliner even though the Prophet forbade it. However, because nothing is written in the

Qur'an about such things, Islamic scholars and ordinary Muslims debate these issues constantly.

At school, the *hijabat* used *haram* and *halal* liberally, especially when one's modesty was in question. The students argued about what was *haram* when something was called into question, and advice was often sought from people such as Saba who was respected for her knowledge of the Qur'an and the Hadith (recorded words, actions, sanctions of the Prophet Muhammad).[3] Girls who were pious or wanted to appear pious did not do or say anything that was likely to be considered *mahkru*. In fact, except for some girls who studied and read the Qur'an, the category *mahkru* was not known or well understood by most girls and boys. For the *hijabat*, most of life fell under *haram* or *halal*, and when scripture did not provide an answer, there was always what they called the Yemeni "folk Islam," occult beliefs (and/or magic) that helped explain and remedy problems.

Arranging school life into religiously motivated textual categories gave the *hijabat* the opportunity to maintain Yemeni social status and norms within the confines of school. Yet, school also gave the girls the chance to stretch home- and community-imposed limits. For example, unlike most teenagers, the *hijabat* were often not allowed to listen to American rock or pop music (in the *mahkru* category), and they were also not allowed to read teen magazines, or anything that might be sexually explicit or imply sexuality. At school, however, whereas the *hijabat* and some of the boys were familiar with the movies that teachers discussed in class—in general, girls in the Southend were not allowed to go to the movies. There was a significant amount of underground reading that took place during lunch, the most social event of the day. I observed that the active engagement with text that took place outside the classroom was not usually present in relation to subject matter within the classroom because the girls often avoided openly discussing taboo topics. In fact, the *hijabat* sometimes refused to participate in watching films or discussing texts if the content was risky, meaning that it crossed a certain religious or cultural boundary. This lack of engagement in the classroom usually occurred in the presence of the boaters, and the *hijabat* had to maintain a proper social performance while the teacher tried to engage the class in the text. Socially the classroom was still an oasis for the *hijabat*, but different rules applied under specific conditions, and therefore their experiences in class were not uniform.

The merging of identity and literacy was quite complex and multifaceted in all of the contexts the *hijabat* inhabited. In their cafeteria cluster of tables, which was buffered by non-Arab students against the Yemeni American boys and boaters, the girls brought forth their contraband: teen magazines, potential yearbook pictures which could be seen only by them and would not be published, and fable-like poems and stories (such as chain letters) about girls who misbehaved. They gossiped around these texts, sharing personal information about their marriages, their families, the men they would like to marry (often in opposition to the ones to whom they were engaged or married), and their friends. During one such instance, both Aisha and Layla, two eleventh graders, suggested that I read *Princess* by Jean Sasson (1992) because "then [I will] really understand what it can be like to be them." This is a popular biography about the tragedies experienced by a Saudi Arabian princess who manages to escape her family and country to tell her story. Both Layla and Aisha identified strongly with the woman in the story and talked about her at length. This was not a book they openly discussed or read at home because, as Saba noted, "It makes Islam and Muslims look bad." All of the *hijabat* in this study reiterated that there is a difference between religion and culture. They argued that Princess Sultana's story by Sasson is a story about culture and not about religion: "there's only one true Islam and that's in the Qur'an, and not in that book," Saba said firmly.

The distinction made by the girls between religion and culture is an important one. It means that, to them, although their religion and their Holy Book cannot be questioned, their culture and cultural acts can. For instance, when the *hijabat* were upset or angry with family decisions about education or marriage, they were very careful to blame it on Yemeni culture and not on Islam. According to them, religious texts sanction meaning, but people were likely to misinterpret words and actions found in the Qur'an, and thus the girls limited their public discourse and interaction with others in order to protect themselves. It is easy to see, then, the significance of the relatively safe classroom or the isolated cluster of *hijabat* within a crowded cafeteria. Those places offered a haven for sharing secret texts, texts that were American and that represented American values. Sometimes, however, these texts reinforced Yemeni cultural values. Here is an example about dating taken from my field notes:

I sit with Amani and the other girls during lunch. A poem written in English from the Internet is passed around the table about a girl who goes out with a boy even though her parents don't allow her to date and expect her to be at a school dance that night. The boy has been drinking heavily and crashes into another car. At the hospital, the girl asks the nurse to tell her parents that she's sorry. The nurse doesn't say anything as the girl dies. It turns out that the car into which the girl and her boyfriend crashed was occupied by her parents, who were both killed instantly. All the girls around the table react to this poem with loud exclamations of "*haram!*" They say that hurting their parents through their actions is forbidden. They admire the girl for taking a risk, but they all agree that it's better not to take such a risk and that "religion knows what's right."

The poem is folded and put away and is shared again later in the classroom with other girls.

The conversation about dating illustrates the significance of private spaces (a small cluster of girls in a large cafeteria) within the school, and it reinforces the teachings of the Qur'an. It also re-creates, bridges, and subverts different cultural norms and is therefore a good example of in-betweenness. As such, it also allows the girls to adapt pragmatically and hypothetically through text to a possible American social situation in which they realistically cannot take part. Private spaces were places and times during which the *hijabat* could voice their concerns, reify their beliefs, and sometimes put their doubts to rest. Public spaces (the cafeteria in general or the hallways), however, were indexed only by culturally laden roles and by religious texts spoken in Arabic or in the English translation, which was not typical of everyday American English speech. For example, some girls not only memorized the Qur'an in Arabic, but could also recite it in English. In other words, throughout the day and regardless of teachers' disapproval, the girls' talk was peppered with Arabic and English excerpts of the Qur'an, and the use of *haram* and *halal* was rampant. At the same time, the *hijabat* found moments during the school day to address topics and issues that were never discussed at home or in their community. The combination of religious textual reference and the clandestine quality of the *hijabat*'s use of nonreligious texts was unique to Cobb High.

Even though the *hijabat* claimed that their culture is independent of their religion, the evidence suggests that the two were intertwined in very elaborate ways. In fact, during an interfaith roundtable (Diversity Day) organized by the high school administration to improve relations between Arab and non-Arab students, when the students were invited to depict pictorially who they are, without exception, every Muslim student (eighteen out of forty-three students) drew a crescent and a star, symbols of Islam. None of the non-Arab students drew a religious symbol. If culture can be defined as performance according to both Goffman and Gee, then so can religion, which is a very specific set of symbolic actions. Geertz (1973), who has written about religion as a cultural system, defines it in the following fashion: "*(1) a system of symbols which acts to (2) establish powerful, pervasive, and long-lasting moods and motivations in men by (3) formulating conceptions of a general order of existence and (4) clothing these conceptions with such an aura of factuality that (5) the moods and motivations seem uniquely realistic* (italics in original, 90)." Not only were the *hijabat* visibly symbolic of their religion because of their dress, but they also embodied their religion with their actions and speech. For example, to Saba, religion was her life, and she talked the talk of militant Muslims:

"Islam has permanent solutions to primary problems." Saba, like all the *hijabat*, strove for a state of grace in her daily life, especially as she struggled to persuade her family to allow her to marry a young Black man who had converted to Islam. She retreated into the text of the Qur'an not only for spiritual reasons but also as a means of protection and power against her family's racial prejudice. By embodying the work of the Qur'an, she did not think that her family could hurt her. The text sanctioned her relationship to the young man even if her culture and family would not.

Reading the Qur'an, as Saba did each day or as Layla did with her father each night, led to three results that relate to Scribner's metaphors: being more knowledgeable about the contents of the Qur'an and therefore more respected by one's family and community, reaching a state of grace by virtue of the fact that reading it endows a spirituality or holiness, and empowering oneself against culturally biased acts. In fact, parents took pride in the fact that their sons and daughters (but especially their daughters) read the Qur'an and prayed. At a school-parent meeting about school violence, one father praised his son's success (a high GPA) in school but chose to describe his daughter's success at being prayerful: "She prays more than I do." In other words, although most of the Yemeni families desired both their male and female children to know the Qur'an and to pray, these characteristics were especially valued in girls because they reflected the family's honor. It was the girls' responsibility to maintain religious values, thus reinforcing a gendered notion of religion. The girls knew this and were genuinely involved in their religious practice, but they were also cognizant of the power one assumed with the thorough knowledge of the Qur'an. If reading the Qur'an incited a state of spiritual grace and power, reading other texts allowed the *hijabat* to adapt and become part of American social and cultural life. This was most easily done at Cobb High School, where the interaction among public and private spaces allowed the girls to maintain cultural and religious norms and to indulge in the same texts, both oral and written, that other non-Arab students did.

Music: The Text of Parties

As a contrast to school life and reading the Qur'an, the *hijabat* enacted cultural and/or religious performance through texts in other social settings. Parties, which often took place within the Southend, were segregated according to gender, and the most controversial text was the music to which the girls listened or danced. Parties were often organized around birthdays and weddings. The girls printed out invitations (written in Arabic and English), which were passed out at school. For weddings, everyone in the Yemeni community was invited. These were important occasions and the entire Yemeni community knew about them. Even though parties took place in the privacy of Yemeni homes and were segregated by gender, they did in fact manifest in-betweenness in concrete ways, through clothing, talk, and music. For instance, most of the *hijabat* removed their scarves and *abayas*, revealing the American clothing—jeans and shirts—which were quite tight. Their hair, although long, was done in the latest fashion: straight or up with wisps of hair around the face. Some of the young married women did not remove their scarves and talked instead about the lyrics in the songs, describing them as *haram* because of the sexual messages in them. Most of the high school girls could not listen to this music at home and dared not tell their parents that they did sometimes at parties. Other girls openly opposed the music and remained covered. Saba, who wore very tight outfits at parties and who was proud of her figure, had turned away from regular music. Her explanation, which follows, reflects and represents other girls' perceptions, misgivings, and doubts about both American and Arab music: "I used to listen to regular music such as, you know, FM98 and tapes and stuff. But I stopped and now I listen to only Islamic music. And Islamic music is only, is only the drum but nowadays there's so many groups of talented Muslims, like rappers, singers, that the music is so beautiful that you can really dance to it."

Saba explained further that there are American or Western musicians and singers who make music to which she can listen because it is based on Islamic teachings. She gave singer Cat Stevens as an example and shared with me a newspaper article about him in which he explains the reasons for his conversion (Stevens n.d.).

> So like, cause from before, the music wasn't, I mean, you could only listen to it, you couldn't really dance it. But now they became more talented. Like there's this one guy, his name was, his name is, one guy that you're probably familiar with. Cat Stevens, a British rock star. Well, now he converted to Islam and he makes his own. His name now is Yusuf Islam and he is so talented. Like his music is so nice. He has these songs for little kids and they only do with the drum but you won't think it's the drum. You'll think it's other music too. But it's the way he uses other drums, different types of drums and they make different kinds of sounds and he makes sounds with his vocal chords so it makes it look like real nice.

In effect, Saba listened to a hybrid type of music, music that is composed of Islamic teachings and Western rock. Again, in-betweenness characterized the music and musical texts to which the *hijabat* listened, danced, and sang. Saba pointed out that she listened to Islamic music because it connected both American and Yemeni cultural and religious spaces:

It's Islamic music but it's American. Some is [from the Middle East], like the ones I found, like the ones that's Arabic but there is . . . usually the ones I buy, the American music is about the people that converted. These three rappers, Joshua, Jesse, and . . . converted. And they're real talented rappers. They're called Sons of the Crescent. And they have like really good rap and like dealing with Islam and to better yourself in the future and better yourself in this world. It's really like, it's mainly rap that doesn't concern all the negative . . . you know, these, about women or this and this and that. Things that shouldn't be said.

Saba and most of the other *hijabat* did not listen to other types of American music because of the possible negative consequences to their reputations.

Because I, sometimes you can say probably like if there's, from the olden days, it's a nice, decent song. Innocent, it deals about like love, it's nice, it's beautiful. Because nowadays, I find that music nowadays is very distracting in a way where they have like things that, I don't know. I'm a very modest person and I don't like to hear like I wanta, you know, this and this and that. Because I don't, I don't think that's modesty and I just, I prefer to listen to something I can benefit from. And I prefer to listen to something that won't be held against me in a way like . . . you know, cause you control what you hear, you control what you see, you control what you say. So if I can control to hear something good than negative, then why not. The main music nowadays is not innocent, not decent.

Music among the *hijabat* served a dual purpose: it helped connect American and Yemeni life more concretely, and it preserved cultural and religious standards for good behavior, such as modesty, and control over one's actions. The *hijabat* listened to other music but not openly, and they certainly did not talk about it at school. Nouria said, "I cover my ears on the bus home, if the music is 'specially bad and the boaters are staring at me." Because parents did not usually approve of American music (and the Imam, the religious leader at the mosque, was against it), the *hijabat* compromised by listening to in-between music. This type of music often included Arabic and English lyrics and sometimes French ones. The music had a fast beat, but it contained musical influences from the Middle East or North Africa that were immediately recognizable as Arab and were therefore deemed appropriate by the girls, even if their parents disagreed. Within the basement spaces at parties, the girls enjoyed this music without worrying about being either too American or not American enough.

Weddings were another type of special occasion during which the *hijabat* indulged in unrestricted behavior and listened to different types of music and in-between lyrics. At school, the girls talked of nothing else but the upcoming wedding, whether the bride and groom were cousins, whether the marriage would be consummated during the night of the party. This talk was preceded by the bride handing out invitations, writ-

بسم الله الرحمن الرحيم
ومن آياته أن خلق لكم من أنفسكم أزواجاً
لتسكنوا إليها وجعل بينكم مودةً ورحمةً
صدق الله العظيم

السيد ⬛⬛⬛⬛   ⬛⬛⬛⬛⬛

وعائلته   **وعائلته**

يتشرفون بدعوتكم لحضور حفل زفاف ولديهما

صفاء ♡ **جبر**

وذلك في تمام الساعة السادسة من مساء يوم الأحد الموافق ١ تشرين الثاني ١٩٩٨

للرجال: في قاعة ستيفانس بانكويت هول • للنساء: في قاعة هيرتيج مانور

Mr. ⬛⬛⬛⬛⬛⬛ and Family &
Mr. ⬛⬛⬛⬛⬛ and Family
request the honour of your presence
at the wedding reception of their children

Safa   &   Gabr

On Sunday, the 1st of Noveber 1998 at 6:00 in the evening
For Men: Stefan's Banquet Hall
⬛⬛⬛⬛⬛⬛⬛⬛
For Ladies: Heritage Manor
⬛⬛⬛ • ⬛⬛⬛

ويعفروركم يتم الفرح والسرور

Figure 4. Wedding Invitation

ten in both Arabic and English script, to all of the Yemeni girls at school. These invitations were symbolic of the bride's new status and success as a young Muslim woman. The girls pored over the invitations throughout the school day, and then showed and read them to their mothers. In this fashion, the news of a wedding spread quickly and efficiently. A wedding was a community affair in the Southend, and generally everyone was invited. Because many families were related and/or had village affiliations in Yemen, it was taken for granted that everyone would send someone from the family to the wedding. The example of an invitation in Figure 4 begins with a short prayer in Arabic praising God and is followed by the announcement of marriage and its locations in both Arabic and English.[4] The celebration is to take place in two different places, one for men and the other for women. At the bottom of the invitation, the families requested in Arabic that small children be left at home, although it was expected that children would come with their parents. The wedding invitation is an example of an in-between text in both language and form. It is clearly symbolic of the girls' literacy adaptation to the commonly enacted wedding invitation genre in the United States. This is not a prevalent practice in Yemen, where many of the girls were betrothed.

At least 200 women attended one of the weddings to which I was invited (see Figure 4). They danced the *debka* (a line dance) and couples belly danced. Each girl danced with the bride—hand and hip movements to the beat of the music. One of the girls commented that dancing to flute music is *haram* because "it makes people do things," yet the women and girls danced to many kinds of music throughout the evening. Every time the (male) manager of the hall walked in to check that all was well, the women would hurry to cover their heads, sometimes with the table linens if the *hijab* was not immediately available. When the groom came back at 8:30 P.M. to cut the cake, all the women covered for the duration. There was no advance warning, so there was a flurry of activity in getting heads covered. Throughout the celebration, it was evident that a conflict over music had ensued near the audiotape player, and the *hijabat* soon left their table to take part in the argument. The older women wanted traditional Yemeni instrumental music so that they could line dance, and the younger women wanted fast Arabic music and Raï music. For example, one of the songs to which the girls wanted to listen, "Aïcha" by Khaled, has a combination of French and Arabic lyrics.[5] The older women refused to dance to it and the younger women refused to dance to traditional Yemeni songs. In the end, a variety of songs were played, and each group of women danced to what they considered appropriate songs.

It is clear that weddings and parties offered special social and intertextual opportunities to the *hijabat*. In these situations, the girls' performance were private ones, where dancing and a variety of talk about school, Yemen, the bride's wedding night experience with her husband, and listening to music could take place without serious infringement upon their public reputations. The Discourse surrounding the various texts—music, print, or talk—can be characterized as in-between or a hybrid of two cultures and languages. Furthermore, the locality of this performance was expressed through states of dress. The *hijabat* were always wearing both Yemeni/Muslim and American clothing (Western clothing under their loose dresses). This was one way they adapted to being both Yemeni and American without disgracing themselves in their community. This setting also gave them a sense of power. In being able to remove certain layers of clothing, they could express themselves differently and more openly and engage in taboo topics with other women from the community. Their appearance was dependent on the context, both temporal and situational, of the performative event, such as a dance or talk about relationships. Conflicting ways of being were resolved by the adoption of certain musical texts to the exclusion of others or a blending of texts. This facilitated life at home and school and empowered their sense of selfhood in multiple contexts.

The Texts of Arabic School

Arabic or Islamic schools have a long history. The golden age of Islam (AD 750–1150) was marked by the establishment and maintenance of a large network of educational institutions, including Islamic schools (Shamsavary, Saqeb, and Halstead 1993). Classical Islamic education was organized into six types of schools, all of which were primarily religious and most of which taught mainly boys.[6] In the Southend, Arabic school was a blend of the *maktab* school, which focuses on reading, writing, and manners, and the *masjid* school, which combines learning with religious education (see Sarroub 2000). Arabic school was organized according to gender and ethnicity and was located in the mosque. There were several Arabic schools in the Arab community of Detroit, but in the Southend, because of the predominance of Yemeni in the community, almost all of the students were Yemeni while the Lebanese and Iraqis attended other schools. The boys entered from one side of the mosque and the girls from the other. They were taught separately, and the girls had women teachers while the boys were taught by men. The girls were always covered from head to toe in *abayas* or very loose long shirts and pants and the *hijab*, whereas the boys generally wore Western clothing, but never shorts. (As a visitor in the mosque, I was also expected to keep my head covered with a scarf and to wear modest clothing.) Arabic school included grades K–7 and met on the weekends from 8:30 in the morning until noon for instruction, after which lectures were scheduled. Each grade was organized by literacy level in Arabic rather than by age, so some of the *hijabat* such as Nouria, a tenth grader, were in the fourth grade. Each grade level had one room, and the small rooms were quite overcrowded. The desks stood against one another, making it almost impossible to stand. Anyone from the Yemeni community could register for Arabic school, and therefore there were often students of various ages at each grade level. If the girls failed a grade, they repeated it until they passed. Each morning before classes began, the teachers, who were Yemeni, Egyptian, and Iraqi, met in the teachers' room. They sat on chairs arranged along the perimeter of the room, facing the principal's desk. When the bell rang the teachers went to their respective classes. After midmorning recess, the teachers changed rooms as they switched from teaching Arabic to religion or vice versa. The students remained in the same rooms. This organization was modeled on schools in the Middle East and in Europe. The teachers move from class to class, whereas the students remain in the same room.

All of the instruction revolved around reading, writing, and the Qur'an. In effect, the students were taught to read and write in Arabic so that they could read the Qur'an, and in the upper grades the Qur'an was used as the main textbook. In the lower grades teachers helped the students memorize various verses from the Qur'an. Oral production, recitation, and listening were emphasized in all grades. Importantly, because Arabic vocabulary is based on a three-letter root system to which affixes are attached, much time was spent learning different roots in the younger grades. For example, in the second grade, the teacher passed out a worksheet on which were listed sets of three letter sounds out of order, and the students were required to recognize the letters and the words they made. So the sounds /th/, /h/, and /b/ make the word *thahaba*, meaning "to go." The children learned that any word with these three sounds in that order will have one basic meaning, "going." Other exercises include syntactic sequencing and conjugation of verbs. The upper grades focused more on grammar, such as learning the parts of speech by rhyme, and they spent most of their time reading the Qur'an and memorizing it.

Instruction at Arabic school was all teacher centered. The students did not address their teachers by name but as "Teacher" or "Moualima." Because the classrooms were so overcrowded and it was so easy for the girls to talk to one another, the teachers usually yelled at the top of their voices during the lessons. In fact the *hijabat* were much louder and laughed more in Arabic school than they did at their public high school. The teachers were often aghast at their behavior and became harsher, calling the girls donkeys or camels in front of the whole class. Literacy instruction took the form of the teacher telling the girls what to do and how to do it with little opportunity for discussion or questions. For assessment, the teachers gave the girls homework such as grammar exercises and verses from the Qur'an to memorize for the next class. Each month, the upper grades took an oral exam, which consisted of reciting from memory different parts of the Qur'an. The *hijabat* often grew impatient with this type of instruction and constantly criticized the teachers for their lack of innovation. But there was little they could do during literacy instruction. However, during religious instruction, they tended to ask many questions about the text and demand an explanation from their teachers. This was distinctly different from classroom instruction at Cobb High, where questioning the text and the author was taken for granted because the teachers usually asked questions. In the context of the Qur'an, the *hijabat* were willing to accept it as the word of God, yet they wondered at the reasons behind their religious practices. For instance, a seventh grader in her late teens asked the teacher why she could not wear a ring on her index finger. The teacher explained that wearing a ring on that finger is *mahkru* because that finger is used during prayer and signified one God. Therefore it is better if it is not adorned.

Religious instruction in Arabic school was characterized by a more open, teacher-centered environment and by the chanting of various sections of the Qur'an. This was especially so at the upper grades, where some of the *hijabat* were young mothers. There was more discussion that was generally led by the questions the students asked, although the teachers definitely transmitted all new knowledge. The teacher reminded the *hijabat* in Arabic and broken English to wear their scarves wherever they went and to pray five times so as to be good role models to the younger girls. Following are excerpts taken from my field notes of a fourth-grade classroom during which one teacher lectured and led a discussion on the *hijab* and modesty.

After chanting a verse about charity in Arabic, the teacher asks the class in Arabic and English, "If someone asks you why you wear a scarf and why you're covered, what do you say? You may say it's because of my religion." The teacher then makes an analogy. She says that "expensive chocolate is covered—in olden times good, expensive chocolate was covered. Allah created feelings in a man. Even if a woman is completely covered, a man can smell her perfume and his feelings will cause him to harm her. We have to cover ourselves. We have to protect ourselves like candy to keep the flies away. In the old days, in the U.S., there was less rape because women wore long dresses and skirts and this kept men from raping women. *Little House in the Prairie, Dr. Quinn* are examples of women who cover themselves and avoid harm. Girls today should cover for the same reason. Among women, women have to cover themselves from waist to knee, or in some cases, from chest to knee. In front of men everything must be covered, like expensive chocolate." The girls listen to what the teachers say with avid interest, but they do not all look convinced.

The teacher was obviously interested in the girls' safety, and by using examples from the American media and Muslim teachings, she interacted with the girls with a mixture of in-between texts. Her words carried a greater import in the context of religious instruction, and her use of popular media to persuade the girls of her viewpoint helped her identify with their daily lives. During one class a young woman asked if a bride should pray on her wedding day. The teacher replied, "Yes, and her wedding night, too, before her husband even kisses her. He should too. Everything should be *baraka* [good] and not harm on the wedding night." The teacher said that in the old country many new brides died on their wedding nights because they were so afraid of what was about to happen, so it was better to pray beforehand. Almost as an after-thought, the teacher commented that the death of so many brides is the reason grooms are allowed to marry relatives of the bride.

The *hijabat* learned and improved their Arabic, but they also heard and learned lessons that were not easily reconciled with those they learned at their public high school or through the American media. The oral and written texts with which the *hijabat* engaged allowed them to connect their religious practice to their identities as teenagers, but these also positioned them as powerless girls whose femininity and education could be a liability. For example, Nouria explained that her goals were at odds with those her male peers had for her. "The Arabic boys, I guess, want [us] to follow the old tradition. You know, don't talk to boys. . . . You're not supposed to be in school. You're supposed to be home cook-ing and cleaning and raising a family." In some ways, the teachers at Arabic school supported this view. According to these teachers, reading the Qur'an and chanting verses present an antidote to the influences of the outside world. In Scribner's sense of literacy as social practice, the discursive reading of the Qur'an empowered the girls with social and intellectual grace, but it paradoxically reified their marginality as mem-bers of American public schooling and society.

Muhathara

In addition to certain literacy practices within the home, such as reading the Qur'an or knowing it well enough to argue one's case during con-flict (such as marriage), one of the most salient textual experiences within the home was the reading and paying of bills. Every girl I met while in the field had the responsibility of informing her parents of incoming information in English and in Arabic. One of the *hijabat*, Aisha, for example, kept records and did the accounting for the rental properties her father managed in the neighborhood. The *hijabat* were aware of their parents' financial status because the parents relied on their children to read and write for them. The girls also followed the academic progress of their siblings and were responsible for ensuring their success in school by helping them with homework. In general, they helped their male siblings before turning to their own homework. Therefore, in order for these Yemeni families to survive in the United States, their daughters' (sons usually worked outside the home) knowl-edge of English and Arabic was crucial. These literacy tasks, characterized by Scribner as adaptation, enabled the Yemeni families to fulfill mundane tasks such as signing papers sent home from school or paying the electricity bills. Yemeni parents, however, also encouraged their daughters to be as versatile in Arabic as they were in English. Consequently the *hijabat* also attended Arabic school till the seventh grade, and they did this on Saturdays and Sundays. Some of the girls also attended *Muhathara* (lectures) and discussions organized by women in the community. Arabic school and *Muhathara* emphasized knowledge of the Arabic language and religious education and morals. In both of these settings, reading, writing, and recitation of text from memory were key practices, and because parents were fearful that their daughters would become "American," they insisted on such instruction for as long as possible before marriage.

Muhathara was a unique space for the *hijabat*. It was a time and place for learning and socializing within the context of reading. The lectures, which a few groups of girls attended, took place either at the mosque or in a private home. The ones at the mosque functioned much more like a traditional lecture, where a woman speaker addressed women's issues in front of an audience, and the audience participated in a discussion at the end. The *Muhathara* held in someone's home, however, was quite different. In the Southend, I was introduced by Saba to Mrs. Bouzain, a woman who led Saba's lecture group. Once a week on Mondays, five to eight high school *hijabat* and young women (some of whom had dropped out of school) from the community gathered in Mrs. Bouzain's basement from five till seven in the evening. The girls arrived and removed their shoes, and because it was time for evening prayer at sunset, they found a quiet corner and prayed before the lecture/discussion began. After the early evening prayers, the lecture began. Each of the girls brought something specific to read from the Qur'an or from a book on Muslim religious conduct. This group functioned much like a book club, but reading or reciting text aloud was emphasized and was followed by a lecture on morality. During one meeting, Saba began the lecture by reading a prayer from the Qur'an. Mrs. Bouzain mouthed the prayer silently with her eyes closed as Saba read. Then Saba recited the Hadith in Arabic and its translation in English. This particular Hadith dealt with being thankful. Mrs. Bouzain proceeded to explain the Hadith, its meaning, and why expressing thanks is important. She admonished the girls in English and Arabic, "You should not be as you are in school. . . . You should bring your hearts to Allah. You're teenagers and you love life, but you have to be serious. In the Arab community, you have to be like a queen. When you walk, people will watch you walk and talk about you." Mrs. Bouzain reiterated the girls' biggest fear: being watched by community members. Because she had daughters at

Cobb High, Mrs. Bouzain understood that the girls were much more open and perhaps less vigilant about their reputations while at school. Therefore, she used Saba's reading from the Qur'an as a segue into a lecture on modesty and good behavior. Mrs. Bouzain exclaimed, "a girl is like glass. If you break it, you can't put it back."

Muhathara gave some of the *hijabat* the opportunity to socialize, but within a strictly textual and religious context. There was no room in this setting for outsiders who did not want to learn the Qur'an. Although I had inquired about the meetings, I was not invited to attend until my second year in the community, when it was established that I wanted to learn more about reading the Qur'an in this context and could be trusted to participate accordingly. *Muhathara* was also a haven for the girls because they trusted Mrs. Bouzain to keep secret their confidences. Although there was an explicit emphasis on recitation and the Qur'an, much more took place implicitly during these meetings.

Muhathara provided an occasion for textual inquiry and response. The *hijabat* felt they could talk to Mrs. Bouzain because she had daughters their age in their school and, importantly, because she was learned. Unlike many of the women in the community, she could read and write in Arabic and recite the entire Qur'an. She had achieved the state of grace and power into which the girls wanted to enter. She was a teacher to them and a friend who did not betray them to their parents. In Mrs. Bouzain's basement and in the context of reading from the Qur'an, one could openly discuss the in-betweenness the girls experienced in and out of school. Although the girls did not disagree with the text of the Qur'an, they sought to understand it in the context of their daily lives.

Muhathara was important for another reason. In a world of fast-paced multimedia, the sanctity of the Qur'an was preserved both emotionally and intellectually, as well as physically. Following, I have included an excerpt from my field notes. It illustrates the powerful connection the *hijabat* made between purity of mind and body. Reading was delimited in unusual ways that suggest a clear link between the purity of the Book and those who read it. This excerpt also shows the intertextual nature of reading, religious talk, and gossip within the group.

At Mrs. Bouzain's the girls recite *surat* (verses from the Qur'an) one after the other in round-robin fashion and refer to the text only when they forget the words. The Qur'an is passed around but Saba doesn't touch it. I volunteer to read and the girls inquire if I can touch it. I don't understand until they ask if I am "clean." I realize, then, what they mean. I nod, and I read the text in Arabic, while Saba recites next from memory. . . . Purity and "touching" is the next topic of conversation. We talk about why the girls don't shake the principal's hand at school. "Touching," Saba says, "is disrespectful and [she] shouldn't have to lose respect for herself by shaking a man's hand just because he's Dr.

Principal. . . ." We talk about the scarf. Mrs. Bouzain says, "When a woman covers herself, she respects herself. She feels better about herself, more secure. When she's covered, she's pure."

Within the repeated Monday event of *Muhathara*, the *hijabat* constructed a routine: late afternoon prayer, recitation of text, lecture from Mrs. Bouzain, gossip and discussion, and conversation with gossip during dinner. The pattern did not change and became more significant as the *hijabat* continued to meet. In effect, *Muhathara* became a system of communicative forms, or genres. In describing genre as dynamic, fragile, provisional, and plastic, Freedman and Medway (1994) point to the social interplay between text and context. Clearly, prior knowledge, such as knowing the Qur'an, served to shape the genres of *Muhathara*. Interestingly enough, genres have boundaries or limits that make them recognizable (e.g., a wedding invitation or one of the verses in the Qur'an), but these boundaries are permeable, allowing for individual or group appropriation within specified contexts. According to this view of genre, the composition of texts, oral or otherwise, becomes a social process, whereby knowledge is created and re-created. In the case of the *hijabat*, they learned something new every Monday night by attending *Muhathara*, but the system by which they communicated remained consistent as did their intention. Bazerman (1994), in his analysis of U.S. patents, has thoughtfully described this form of enactment of genre as "the intention, the recognition of the intention, the achievement of the intention with the coparticipation of others, and the further actions of others respecting that achievement" (82). Bazerman's observation accurately describes the intentioned realization of the interactions set in motion every Monday night by the *hijabat* and Mrs. Bouzain.

It is clear from the example of one of the *Muhathara* meetings at Mrs. Bouzain's house that the *hijabat*'s culture and religion had a tremendous impact on their school lives. Many teachers at Cobb High simply did not understand the cultural and social limits within which these Muslim girls negotiated their American and Yemeni selves. It is fair to say that community and family values (both implicit and explicit ones) sometimes differed significantly from those at school. Literacy as social practice during *Muhathara* became meaningful because it endowed a state of spiritual grace upon the girls and also allowed them to talk openly about their religious or cultural concerns. This was very different from conversation at lunch around magazines or other contraband. The conversations during *Muhathara* were characterized by the girls as more intellectual and religious. They saw the reading of the Qur'an and the conversation that ensued around the readings as knowledge to be learned rather than just talk among friends or "stuff you learn at school." These groups of girls grappled with disturbing religious and moral issues for a purpose: to stay true and pure to Islam, to show their community that they were good Muslim girls, and to converse openly about risky topics that they could not openly discuss in school or elsewhere. For example, the girls discussed wearing gloves so that they would have no skin contact with male administrators or teachers during school award or graduation ceremonies. On the one hand, *Muhathara* was an empowering space because it offered the *hijabat* a venue for both social and intellectual activity. On the other hand, as with Arabic school, this setting also marginalized them by mitigating their femininity to the expected religious and cultural standards of the Yemeni community. For example, Layla spoke candidly about what was expected of her: "They [parents] think . . . Arabic girls are not supposed to have like, they try to seclude us from anything. Like from guys or from anything. They don't want us to have like the natural feeling of anything. You know. That's why they'll be like, you know, never talk to guys. Put your head on the floor. Like when I was in the mosque, I remember like, like the teacher, she'll tell us that you know, when you walk in the hallways, you should have your head on the ground. Because the guys don't look at, they'll look at you and they'll get evil thoughts." As such, she and the other *hijabat* maintained a rather fragile balance between their Yemeni and American identities through the social practice of textual inquiry.

Many ethnographies, monographs, and histories have been written about people who occupy the often figurative and sometimes physical borderlands (among them Carger 1996; Hall 1995; Raissiguier 1994). I chose in-betweenness as a concept for the *hijabat* because it ties together notions of text, literacy, space, gender, ethnicity, and identity. It is also a concept that some of the *hijabat* used when I asked them to describe themselves within their Yemeni and American worlds. In-betweenness attempts to create real or imagined boundaries to describe what people do to survive and get along with one another on a daily basis. The use of such a concept demarcates, however peripherally, an epistemological if not situational marker for understanding home and school worlds as a set of relationships in the *hijabat*'s lives. As such, in-betweenness is a nebulous concept, but it is a useful analytical lens through which various literacies can be understood. The implication of this characterization is that for in-betweenness to remain in between, it must shift as its borders shift. I suspect that this occurs over time and with each succeeding generation of immigrants. The lives I uncovered while I lived among the *hijabat* in the Southend are among the most dynamic I have ever experienced. The *hijabat* dealt with conflicting visions of literacy on a daily basis. However, they adapted to their situation by adopting an in-between text. This allowed them to perform successfully or to enact cultural norms that were acceptable and valid in the given context. At the same time, however, striving to be both American and Yemeni, boy or girl, could be a struggle. The Discourses that accompanied these identities are complex and complicated, affording the *hijabat* little power but endowing them with grace within public spaces. Knowing the Qur'an and being modest bestowed grace upon the individual. Within the private spaces, whether at school or elsewhere, grace often fell by the wayside as the *hijabat* attempted to connect and adapt their Yemeni selves to their American selves. This could be as easy as shedding a layer of clothing at a party or as difficult as reading a book or poem clandestinely. In either case, the girls were told at *Muhathara* and Arabic school that these actions were wrong and perhaps sinful. Yet, the *hijabat* continued these actions, finding more and more in-between situations within which to live.

Scribner's (1984) work illustrates the importance of varieties of literacies for the survival and socioeconomic success of communities. One example of the enactment of language and cultural competencies that cuts across socioeconomic background and ethnicity in schools and that facilitates textual practices within in-between spaces comes from Moll's funds of knowledge project within working-class Latino populations and their experiences with non-Latino teachers (Moll 1992; Moll, Amanti, and Gonzales 1992; Moll and Gonzalez 1994). Moll (1992) defines funds of knowledge as "the historically accumulated and culturally developed bodies of knowledge and skills essential for household or individual functioning and well-being" (133). The funds of knowledge perspective acknowledges that social class can be an impediment to or a catalyst of learning and achievement. However, "the essential cultural practices and bodies of knowledge and information that households use to survive, to get ahead, or to thrive" (Moll 1992:21) are part of wider social networks and are required by diverse labor markets. In other words, Moll suggests that if schools could find a way to explicitly privilege cultural tools of minority populations, the range of students who could rely on cultural knowledge to engage in successful school practices would be expanded. Therefore schools and teachers would do well to become familiar with these funds of knowledge simply because they represent "a *potential* major social and intellectual resource for the schools" (22). Moll's research illustrates that when schools make attempts to understand the underlying social, cultural, and language networks of the populations they serve, it is more likely that there will be congruence between what content is taught and how it is taught and the students' ability to learn, thus broadening the definitions of privileged cultures and tools to include more than just social class distinctions.

An example of this, although not representative of the funds of knowledge perspective, comes from one of the first research studies conducted on the connection between home and classroom discourse. The researchers observed that there was a mismatch between the teacher's expectations for classroom behavior and her students' (who were Italian Americans) knowledge of the required norms for proper behavior (Shultz, Florio, and Erickson, 1982). Shultz and his colleagues found that although the students' social etiquette was perfectly acceptable at home, it did not meet the expectations of the classroom. They concluded that teachers and researchers should "understand more fully children's socialization into communicative traditions at home and at school, traditions that may be mutually congruent or incongruent" (91). It is clear that researchers who have studied the impact of home cultures and social class on success at home and in school concluded that, although socioeconomic standing is a useful tool, it does not always explain how individuals learn, produce knowledge, and sustain cultural and/or social identities in multiple worlds. Heath (1982), for example, showed that the complex language socialization process is "more powerful than single-factor explanations accounting for academic success" (344). Scribner (1984) points out that "as ethnographic research and practical experience demonstrate, effective literacy programs are those that are responsive to perceived needs, whether for functional skills, social power, or self-improvement. . . . The road to maximal literacy may begin for some through the feeder routes of a vide variety of specific literacies" (18).

The *hijabat* were all highly literate and engaged with their religious text, which pervaded much of their lives. This specific literacy could be both liberating and oppressive. For example, like the *Muhathara*, Arabic school in the Southend used the context of reading to instill fear and mistrust. This had grave consequences. When the girls were told to think of themselves as wrapped chocolate or as fragile glass, the implication was that they did not have power and therefore could be hurt. It is no wonder that they were so frightened of marriage or of talking openly in the school cafeteria. Arabic school did offer them the opportunity to discuss many important issues relating to their religion, and they did so boisterously and with a certain level of irreverence for their teachers, but they also received mixed messages about their status as women, their education, and their futures as workers in the world or the home. Arabic school was an in-between place where the girls interacted intellectually with their teachers. The discourse of Arabic school, much like that of *Muhathara*, was a threatening one, for it positioned the *hijabat* as victims of society, and in some ways, it hindered the negotiation process of living in two worlds. Public school, on the other hand, offered a mixture of possible discourses and certain freedom to choose among them to reach both academic and social success, from classroom content (even if most of it was teacher centered in presentation) to cafeteria conversations around secret poems. It is no wonder that the *hijabat* preferred that space to Arabic school, even though they all agreed that knowing Arabic was important to them and to their families.

It is clear that the *hijabat* negotiated their home and school lives in unique ways. They adapted to a given situation by creating or adopting in-between texts that helped them bridge two cultures. It is important that parents, educators, and researchers as well as policy makers be aware of the texts youth employ to make sense of their world. As I noted in Chapter 2, all too often, most teachers remained ignorant of the girls' community, their religion, and their struggle to be both American and Yemeni. They had no idea how the *hijabat* were positioned and how they were positioning themselves within their various interactions and ritual performances in and out of school. If public schools are to support diversity in their domain, then the teachers and administrators must be aware not only of its existence but also of its manifestation and acknowledge that diverse literacy practices are part of a larger geopolitical way of life. Awareness is the first step toward understanding and perhaps a first step toward a pedagogy of specific literacies, to use Scribner's term, that not only centers on individual students but also privileges those students' communities. As Street (1995) notes, in order to develop better curricula, the wider socioeconomic and political context is integral to the process. Knowing that there are conflicting visions of what it means to be literate and what it means to enact multiple literacies seems to me to be crucial to the development of critically responsive pedagogy and powerful social and academic curricula. In the case of the *hijabat*, who come from low socioeconomic status homes, I found that they managed a demanding academic schedule while they simultaneously performed tasks and lived up to family responsibilities unknown to most adolescents. Yet they did this on the margins and were further marginalized both in their own community and in their school. This prompted them to actively seek ways to succeed in multiple contexts. When I left the Southend, teachers were only beginning to learn about how rich and demanding these girls' lives were in and out of school. As in the example of Saba and her prayer in the car, in-between spaces and texts helped satisfy the demands that the girls faced as they attempted to succeed at being good Muslims, good daughters and wives, and good students. As they continue to navigate home, and perhaps school, spaces I remain optimistic that schools will also experience shifting in-betweenness that will privilege their students' and communities' texts.

Chapter 5

The Tensions Teachers Face: Public Education and Islam

A community, no matter how carefully nurtured and no matter how politically astute and committed to its members, does not sit isolated from the contradictory economic, political, and cultural dynamics of the institutions in which it resides. Nor does it sit isolated from the race, gender, class, and other dynamics of the larger society.

—Michael Apple, *Official Knowledge*

The growing population of Yemeni students at Cobb High led teachers and administrators to carefully consider the dilemmas of cultural pluralism within their school. In particular, it led them to struggle with the issue of accommodating the cultural traditions of Muslim students in general and Yemeni Muslim students in particular. Both at organizational and personal levels, high school and district personnel inevitably met certain challenges that called for conciliatory measures to ensure a sound learning environment for all students. With a growing population (40 percent at the time of my fieldwork) of Muslims, the majority of whom were Arab "newcomers" of Yemeni descent who had little long-term presence in the surrounding neighborhood, Cobb High found itself, from 1997 to 1999, in the middle of cultural and religious strife between the Arab and non-Arab communities. This conflict was occasioned by (or at least encapsulated in) two incidents, one having to do with a districtwide memorandum from the superintendent to principals over a Muslim holiday in April 1997, and the other with a cafeteria food fight on December 2, 1997. Although these incidents escalated tensions among various groups within the school and in the community, teachers at Cobb High had begun the process of unpacking and addressing the tensions among their staff and students long before, in the late 1980s and early 1990s, when the number of Yemeni students soared dramatically, from a miniscule percentage to almost 30 percent, following the war in Lebanon, Yemen's political turmoil, and the Gulf War. The incidents of 1997 served to accelerate [in interesting ways] the course of accommodation already in place, including how teachers and administrators dealt with the cultural, religious, ethnic, and gender tensions that arose as their minority population slowly increased. This chapter is based on an analysis of field observations specifically around accommodative measures; interviews conducted with twenty-two "mainstream" and bilingual program teachers, school counselors, and social workers; as well as a wide array of documents, ranging from districtwide memos to daily school bulletins, school memos, and local newspaper articles.

Formal Accommodation in Historical Context

In 1992, Cobb High School formed the Committee on Cultural Understanding to explore students' perceptions of peer relationships. The committee included the principal and several teachers. Their goal, as stated in a report from an external task force, which was invited to help begin the process of cultural understanding, was to ensure that "students [would] demonstrate an understanding and acceptance of all cultures."[1] The report states that after consultation with the Southend's community center, a multiple-choice and true-false multicultural survey was administered to the class of 1995, all ninth graders, to test their cognitive knowledge of mainstream American, Middle Eastern, Asian, and Hispanic cultures. The following are sample questions from the multicultural survey:

1. An Arab is . . .
   A) anyone from the Middle East
   B) a believer in Islam
   C) a native speaker and writer of Arabic
   D) all of the above

2. What is an "Hispanic"?
   A) a person who speaks Spanish
   B) an American whose native language is Spanish
   C) a person from a Spanish-speaking country
   D) none of the above

4. Lebanon is about the size of which U.S. state?
   A) Texas
   B) North Carolina
   C) Connecticut
   D) California

8. How many countries have Spanish as their official language?
   A) 10
   B) 20

    C) 30
    D) none of the above

26. A kimono is . . .
    A) a garment
    B) a temple
    C) a city
    D) a fruit grown in Asia

36. America is an older nation than China. (T/F)

39. Arabic nations are basically communist nations. (T/F)

46. Generally, compared to Middle Eastern families, U.S. families have fewer children. (T/F)

The survey was administered to 197 students. The mean score (from a possible score of 60) was 28.3, and the range was 8–52. Based on this data the task force observed that, although the survey did not deal with student dispositions, students were uncomfortable with the test procedure. (Some teachers told me they found the survey questions absurd.) The task force recommended that "more interactive student, parent, and community involvement in planning would facilitate strategies that are more student-oriented and owned rather than teacher directed." The task force also noted that Cobb High should consult other schools and districts who had "undergone adaptation" to cultural diversity and that teachers should participate in staff development sessions on cultural diversity and the function of the bilingual program. Finally, they recommended that the district support Cobb High's efforts through policy and funding. In addition to the survey, during the winter of 1993, focus group interviews were held with randomly selected Arab American and non-Arab students regarding their perceptions of their interethnic relationships at school.[2] Based on the combined results of the survey and these interviews, Cobb High began to implement formal and informal curricular strategies to better accommodate the Muslim students and to forge links between the school and the Muslim community, especially the parents.

    The process of accommodation was by no means an easy one. As in British schools, whose largest minority consists of Muslim students, Cobb High initiated a series of reforms, broadly construed as informal and formal curricula (Haw and Hanifa 1998). The formal curriculum included resource material about Muslims, the bilingual program, Friday afternoon leave for religious instruction, consultation and sensitivity to religion, adaptation of the physical education curriculum, and sensitivity to swimming arrangements. The informal measures included dietary accommodation, the establishment of a diversity club, the use of dual language signs within the school, and the recognition of Muslim holidays. To facilitate home and school connections, a community-school liaison was hired in the fall of 1998, and regular consultation with the mosque and community center was implemented. Unlike Britain, which is not as aggressively secular as is the United States with its public schools, prayer facilities and the appointment of Muslim staff were not included in Cobb High's curricular changes.

Although the process of adaptation to the Yemeni population began when the Yemeni from the Southend began to be bussed approximately 6.5 miles to the high school in the late 1980s and early 1990s, the development of more thoughtful accommodation strategies took a serious turn in the fall of 1997, as a result of confusion and misinformation over religious observance. On April 14, 1997, the superintendent of the Dearborn school district sent to all the principals and assistant principals a memorandum in which he stated that Muslim families should be encouraged to delay their holiday celebrations:

> This Thursday, April 17, is an Islamic holyday/holiday commemorating the event when God asked Abraham to sacrifice his son as a test of Abraham's faith.
> While our school district is committed to respecting the religious observances of its children and their families, there is a major consequence if student attendance is abnormally low this Thursday.
> In Michigan law, if a school district's total attendance falls below 75% on any one day, the district forfeits state aid for that day (snow days, or "acts of nature," so to speak, aren't counted, up to a certain point). One day's state aid for us in [Dearborn] is about $340,000. We could avoid this loss by scheduling an extra day of school at the end of the year, but that would obviously require the consent of our employee groups.
> Without being insensitive to the importance of this religious holiday, if there is a way for you to encourage your Muslim families to delay the holiday celebration till the weekend it would be beneficial to our district.
> P.S. Please remember that in order for a religious holiday absence not to count against a student's attendance record, a written parent excuse is necessary, verifying that the absence is for this purpose.[3]

This memorandum prompted a backlash from the Arab community in Dearborn. In response to the protest, two days later, the superintendent sent the principals another memorandum, apologizing for appearing insensitive:

> I have received much criticism today for my previous memo regarding the Muslim holiday, student attendance, and state aid. Some of this criticism has hit you directly as the "messenger" of my message.
> Many of our Muslim staff and parents feel I have been insensitive in suggesting that their holy day can be moved around and postponed till Saturday. It was

suggested that, if December 25 fell on Thursday, this would be like asking students to delay celebrating Christmas until Saturday.

I admit that I was acting somewhat out of ignorance. I had been told that the upcoming Muslim feast was four days in length and thought that the celebration for students could be delayed till the third day, Saturday. I was not aware that the *first* day was the most important and consisted of religious ceremonies in the mosque.

I am sorry if I created a problem for you by asking you to relay my earlier message to students and their families, and I apologize to our Muslim staff and parents if I appeared to be insensitive to the nature and importance of this religious holiday.[4]

These memoranda fueled the mounting tensions between the school and its Arab population just as Cobb High was grappling with issues of integration between Arab and non-Arab students within the building and in the community.

On December 2, 1997, some eight months after the *holyday* fiasco, a fight broke out between an Arab American boy and a non-Arab boy in the cafeteria. In a letter to the mother of the Arab American boy, one of the assistant principals stated that her boy would be suspended for ten days because he had initiated the fight in the hallway by saying to the other boy, "What all you white honkies doing?" to which the other boy took offense and called him an "Arab."[5] This exchange resulted in a fistfight between the two students. The principal stated in the letter that "this happened after a major warning had been given to all students here at Cobb about ethnic slurs or intimidations." The Arab American boy also threatened to "blow up the school" as he was dragged away from the fight.

The "cafeteria incident," as it was subsequently called in all school correspondence and media reports, marked a turning point in Cobb High's short history with its Yemeni population. Much to the surprise of the school and community, at a Board of Education meeting on December 8, 1997, one of the Yemeni American *hijabat* declared that she had been "knocked down, kicked and hit with racial/ethnic slurs" during the fight.[6] These accusations had not been made on the day of the fight, and as one of the assistant principals pointed out in his memorandum, "Several students and staff were astonished at her statements to the Board of Education. Many thought this was less than honest and it has left a bad feeling among staff and students." Cobb High was contacted on December 23, 1997, by the director of Education and Outreach for the American-Arab Anti-Discrimination Committee in Washington, D.C. The superintendent responded to the Washington group with the following explanation:

I have met several times with a group of 18 district staff, including 8 from [Cobb High], to discuss what needs to take place at Cobb (. . . and elsewhere in our school district) to increase the understanding and respect students and adults have for each other. The Cobb members of this group, working independently, have come up with a plan for their school, which plan received the approval and support of the whole faculty at a meeting on January 12, 1998. I am also discussing with our Social Studies department the development of some special teaching units.

. . . I cannot end this letter without asking you to believe me that the information you received about the Cobb cafeteria event is not entirely accurate and that you received some extremely exaggerated reports. I am not proud of what happened there but the vicious scene of mob rule and outright physical aggression against innocent Arab female bystanders is not accurate. Teachers and other cafeteria supervisors who were present at the scene were absolutely dumbfounded to read the allegations contained in your letter.[7]

While the Dearborn School District tried to deal with multiple allegations of wrongdoing from internal and external sources, Detroit area newspaper portrayals included descriptive phrases such as "strife," "ethnic turmoil," "conflict," "understanding is needed," "ethnic fighting," "cultural clash," and "unrest," just to name several of the more prominent themes. Within the walls of Cobb High School, teachers and students struggled in their own negotiations for improvement of relations among the students and faculty, even as their actions mirrored media descriptions. On December 12, 1997, a small group of Arab American students, all of whom were of Yemeni descent and most of whom were *hijabat*, met with teachers and principals to discuss their concerns. Mrs. Barnabey, one of the teachers, shared with me the students' list of grievances as noted by one of the school principals. These grievances dealt specifically with how the principals, the secretaries, and the teachers related to Arab and Arab American students:

Administration:
- Administration says Arabic students are a pain in the neck
- Using words like "you guys" when dealing with situations
- Telling Arabic students to "not push their luck" when asking about their holidays off
- Arabic students get harder discipline than non-Arabic students
- Administrators lie to Arabic students
- Annual Arab/non-Arab fight expected—administrators do not take any actions to avoid it—students know it's coming

Secretaries:
- Secretaries give Arabic students dirty looks when they come into the office
- Secretaries ignore Arabic students when they come into the office

Teachers:
- No teaching of Arabic culture/no mention of Islamic holiday
- Staff makes little effort to force mixing of students—particularly in lab or group

- Arabic students go to teachers to complain and nothing happens
- Teachers do not listen to Arabic students but will listen to non-Arabic students
- Some teachers allow students to say A-Rab and other offensive words without punishment

General Concerns:
- The handling of the cafeteria fight was not done fairly
- Yearbook not representing the Arabic population—yearbook photos getting lost or misplaced.
- There is a lack of understanding of the Arabic culture by students and staff
- Arabic students don't feel welcome in after-school clubs
- When asked the question, [they] named some good teachers who they said treated them with respect, dignity, and appeared to treat *all* students equally[8]

Many items on this list perplexed administrators and teachers alike, whose experiences with the Yemeni and Yemeni American students had made clear that the students, and the girls in particular, could not and would not engage in many academic and social activities at school and/or in class. What was more interesting to teachers and administrators was that the *hijabat* were the students who were the most vocal about making changes in the school to accommodate the Arab and Arab American students. Students such as Saba attended meetings and demanded reform. Unfortunately, in the case of Saba, she alienated several teachers when she called them racist, and the principal had to bar her from attending certain meetings. Based on the meeting regarding the list of grievances and the previous incidents, Cobb High created a plan of action for intervention at three levels: a parent intervention, a student intervention, and a staff intervention.[9] The parent intervention emphasized hiring a community liaison who would meet regularly with community groups; converting English documents into Arabic; providing shuttle services from the Southend to the school during Open House and Parent/Teacher Conferences; and translating the Curriculum Guide, Student Code of Conduct, and other important documents from English to Arabic and other languages if necessary. The student intervention focused on blending students from the two middle schools that feed into Cobb High so that the predominantly Arab American population at one middle school and the predominantly non-Arab students at the other would have an opportunity to adjust to one another earlier; creating an ambassadors group for the orientation of new students in the school; organizing meetings for teachers, administrators, and students around school concerns; increasing involvement in the student leadership area; making curricular objectives changes at the middle school level with reenforcement activities at Cobb; exploring diversity through writing assignments in ninth grade and tenth grade English/humanities courses; forming a "Diversity Club"; and working alongside community centers to educate new immigrant students in some of the more general aspects of American schools. Staff intervention included in-service or school improvement days on diversity education, the practice of heterogeneous grouping and seating charts, and an intervention to improve inappropriate language related to diversity. Following the dispersion of the action plan to community members and school faculty, the principal wrote a memorandum to the faculty in which he once more emphasized the management of students in classrooms:

> At the last Faculty Meeting I spent some time discussing the Action Plan [with] a committee of staff members developed in response to community concerns. At the close of the meeting, consensus was given to implement any and/ or all points listed. We have started the implementation of some items (i.e., increasing student leadership, investigating the formation of a diversity club, routine meetings with students, planning for a new freshmen orientation program). One item that I wanted to emphasize from the action plan is the forced mixing of students whenever classroom activities are occurring. I would like all staff members to take professional responsibility to culturally mix students whenever classroom activities are occurring. The optimum plan would include culturally mixing students in seating charts as well. Your cooperation in this effort will be appreciated.[10]

This memorandum caused much consternation among the teachers who had *hijabat* and Yemeni boys, including boaters, in their classrooms. As I suggested in Chapter 3, segregated seating was important to the *hijabat*, and from that standpoint students then could decide how easily and safely they could partake of the normative classroom practices. Although the students had called for more integration measures within the school, teachers recognized that the reality of classroom life and Yemeni cultural norms would not allow them to freely mix the boys and girls as the principal suggested. Regardless of the institutional efforts made by the school and district, teachers would be caught in the middle, as enforcers of unenforceable measures and as inadvertent agents of American culture.

Teachers and Administrators' Perceptions of the Accommodation Process

Bargaining for grades—why it's not like haggling for beans: A vignette
It's hot. Ali's mother has sent him to the *souk* (market) to buy some beans for tonight's dinner. She tells him not to spend more than what's right. Ali walks around the stalls and hardly pays attention to the men yelling out their wares and prices. He does notice, though, that the prices seem different from yesterday when he was here to buy potatoes. Finally, Ali gets to the bean stand, and

asks the merchant how much for a kilo. He gives Ali a number and Ali shakes his head. Then the haggling begins. Ali says, "C'mon! That's too much. I didn't even pay that much last week. You can do better. You know me. I come here every week." And so it goes for twenty minutes, back and forth, back and forth. It's a game, and Ali tries to outsmart the crafty merchant until they both come to an agreement and Ali gets his kilo of beans. At the end Ali may still have some money left over from what his mother gave him, but not really enough to impress anyone with his bargaining skills.

Ali sits in the back row of the classroom, and he's surrounded by six other Yemeni and Yemeni American boys. This is math and Mrs. Jackson is handing out the graded tests. She's on the other side of the room where all the scarfed girls, five in all, sit together and apart from the other students. All that can be seen of one girl are her eyes. The girls talk quietly in their softly accented Dearborn Arabic English to one another while Mrs. Jackson walks around the room handing out tests and reacting to the smiles and groans with a stoic expression. The boys talk in Arabic teasing each other about being smart and dumb.

Ali gets a C on his test and groans aloud. He follows Mrs. Jackson around the room and says, "Mrs. J, why'd I get a C?

"You didn't study hard enough."

"C'mon, you know me. I study. Change it."

"No, you'll just have to do better next time. It's not the end of the world."

"C'mon, Mrs. J! What'll it take? Give me a B−. I deserve a B−. You know me."

"I told you, Ali, that's your grade."

"C'mon, a C+. You can do that. A C isn't right."

"Ali, go sit down. I told you before that I don't change grades. You and your friends never learn. Just study more."

Ali goes to his seat, his posture stiff and angry. He turns to me and says, "Look, wouldn't you give me at least a B?

"I'm not your teacher, Ali. I'm just shadowing today."

Ali turns to his friends and speaks to them in Arabic, commenting that Mrs. Jackson is a bitch. They all laugh.

It's clear that although Mrs. Jackson doesn't understand what they say, she senses their resentment toward her. She remembers her first experience at the beginning of the year when she acquiesced and changed Sharif's grade. It never stopped. She'd give him two extra points and he'd beg for three more, and so it would go on. She'd almost torn her hair out. No respect, that's what this is. She knows that some other teachers feel the same way. Well, she'd have another story for them today at lunch. As she looks around the room, she thinks to herself, "At least the Arab girls are conscientious. They study hard and always behave." She begins the new lesson on the board.

In the meantime, Asya stares disappointingly at her grade. Another B. It's going to ruin her GPA if she keeps taking this math class. She whispers to her closest friend and cousin, Amina, who got a C, and they both agree that if it's too late to drop they'll switch to a different teacher next semester. Asya says that she'll have to miss two weeks this semester when she has her baby so it's really better to drop if she can so that her GPA doesn't get worse. Amina agrees and says that she'll have to tell her parents that math doesn't really matter when you want to be a nurse.

In the meantime, Ali makes plans for a ride with Sharif after school. Both boys work from 3:30 P.M. to midnight at a restaurant in Greek Town in Detroit. Their grades matter but only to the degree to which it may affect getting their diplomas and graduating on time. Working is what matters.

The bell rings and the students file out of the room noisily. The *hijabat* keep to themselves and the boys push and shove. The non-Arab students do the same, although they don't all file out in boy-girl groups.

The teacher breathes a sigh of relief even as she wonders at the Arab words left hanging in the air as the door shuts.

The vignette is an example of the day-to-day bargaining teachers engaged in with their Yemeni and Yemeni American students. From haggling over grades, to having married and pregnant *hijabat* in class, to implementing a seating arrangement that would accommodate both school mandates and cultural norms—these are just some of the tensions teachers faced each day. Teachers and staff made certain kinds of accommodation to ensure that all their students had the opportunity to succeed in school, but there was a range in their expectations for conformity from and dispositions toward their students.

Teachers at Cobb High School viewed their roles in one of two ways with regard to their relationships with the Yemeni populations. These roles were intimately connected to the teachers' own ethnicity and ties to their own communities. The majority of teachers, all of those who were ethnically non-Arab, described themselves as teachers who have the same expectations of all their students, regardless of ethnicity, and whose main objective is to teach their subjects. This is the classic liberal view of equity—treat all students the same—that characterized American racial dispositions in the 1960s. It is in stark contrast to either multiculturalism or cultural particularism, the more current views of diversity. Overall, these teachers did not see themselves as invested in their students' personal lives and made clear demarcations between school and community and home life. To these teachers, who were predominantly of white and European descent, accounting for differences and similarities in cultural background or gender norms in the classroom intensified their workload, so they categorically shied away from such work intensity (see Apple 1986; Gitlin, Buendia, Crosland, and Doumbia 2003 regarding work intensification). The *hijabat* felt this separation between school and community life and told me that they sometimes "really talked" to or confided in only five non-Arab teachers in the whole building.

The Arab American teachers—most of whom taught in the bilingual program and had very little interaction with the Yemeni American *hijabat*—included the metaphor of being a parent to their students and of feeling a sense of obligation and responsibility toward their Arab and Arab American students in their talk about their students. It should be noted here that not all Arab American teachers welcomed this added responsibility and work intensification, but they understood that in many ways they were indeed surrogate parents and agents of American and Arab cultures to the newcomers, especially because many of their students were illiterate in Arabic and had never been to school before arriving in the United States. As Mrs. Ishmael, one of the bilingual program teachers said, "You know, sometimes I feel I'm part of the family. I mean like a family member. And, usually, these kids, they look at you like, like a father or a mother or a sister, whatever." Another teacher, Mrs. Ali, also reinforced the parent metaphor:

I think they [the Arab community] expect us to teach them the language, the content, manners, because back home, [the] teacher was like a second mom or dad for those students. I think their expectation is the same thing. We send them to you, you are in charge. And I've had, I've had parents where they tell me, listen, if he doesn't listen to you, spank him. Hit him. Like a parent. So, and we do act like parents sometimes, when we sit down and teach them morals and respect and values and you cannot talk like that, it's wrong. You have to go to school. You know, like, like that because we know they're not getting that at home.

Mrs. Ali, as an Arab American teacher of Lebanese descent, accepted the responsibility of being a "parent" to her students in the bilingual program, but she was also troubled by her students' lack of adaptation to American norms. In fact, she was often embarrassed by her students. Her statement that follows illustrates the difficulty she experienced in her role as "parent" and as agent of American cultural norms:

See, now, if I talk to the father, I will say maybe he doesn't understand because he's not good, he's not here so he doesn't see how Americans are and how . . . so he doesn't know, maybe understand. But these kids *are* here. They see Americans, how they are. They are with the Americans. They see how clean they are. How they smell, how they, you know, everything. You know, it's like they are the same thing as their parents. And I have students we have two years, three years, you would expect they would learn something from the way they are here. No. What's here stays the way it is, that's it. I'm gonna dress that way. This is the way I'm gonna smell. This is the way I'm gonna look. No change. This is something I, you know, I was shocked. I mean, I am shocked about. Because when we came here [in the early 1900s], it was different. We didn't shower every day back home. These things were not available for us. But when you took gym, it was mandatory, everybody has to shower. Everybody has to do that. I don't know. And we tell them, you know, you guys gotta be in the mainstream, you know, we don't look bad. We are all, you know, they're gonna think all Arabs are like that. Why you say that, why you do that. You have to change. I mean, you come and, this is, now we are in heaven. In the winter time, it's freezing outside and we can't open the windows. We have 35 students smelling like that, you know how bad it is? You know how embarrassing it is to us when the principal comes into our classroom? Or a teacher comes in the classroom? It's embarrassing. We don't know what to do. And if I open the window, we are freezing. They don't have decent sweaters to wear. And there, some of them come in with the same clothes three, four days a week. The same clothes they're going to work with, same clothes they sleep with, probably the same clothes they're coming to school with. This is a big, and teachers, they raise this problem, during faculty meeting about the hardship.

Mrs. Ali expected her students, the majority of whom were boys, to adapt to American cultural norms from their interaction with their American peers and thus accepted her role as "parent" to help the students become more American. In addition, as an Arab American, she was concerned about her students' images as Arabs among her colleagues and her principal even though she also understood that many of her students were poor and did not have the means or resources "to be clean." The embarrassment she felt along with the need to be a surrogate parent were inner conflicts that she experienced as a teacher in the bilingual program on a daily basis.

Mr. Yasser, also a teacher in the bilingual program, resented being put in the position of "parent" or role model. "They [the Arab community and parents] believe that I should be the role model, the perfect person. Okay? I don't think that's true. . . . I'm too Americanized for them." As an American teacher of Lebanese descent, Mr. Yasser found that he had little in common with his Yemeni students. Like most teachers at Cobb High, teaching this new population meant learning the mores of another culture and adapting his teaching to fit with his students' expectations. His comments point to the notion that there is diversity among Arab Americans. He explained an incident that changed how he would normally conduct informal classroom discussions with the Yemeni boys.

You know, [with] a lot of the kids, when they first came here, I had the worst time in the world. It was such a bad teaching experience because I had never taught Yemenis before. And I had to find out a lot about their culture. Prime example is that I always felt that, okay, the last ten minutes of class we'll speak English. And so like how are you today, you know, everybody one day was like how are you. You know, next day, what did you do last night? Finally, I said well, how's your mom. And how's your mother, the whole class went silent. The kid got very embarrassed and verbally abusive. Why are you asking about my mother? Who are you? And I didn't realize that you don't ask about their mothers. It's like, right. I mean, any Lebanese culture, Syrian culture, you know, you see somebody and you're friends with them, well, how's your mom and dad doing? You know, no qualms about anything. But in this one particular culture, you know, it's different. Even the Iraqis, I can ask the Iraqis, well, how's your mom doing, you know. You meet some of these parents and they're like wonderful. Oh, she's doing good, you know.

The bilingual teachers' experiences with the new immigrant population in their school were challenging, as illustrated by Mr. Yasser's comments. An Arab American himself, Mr. Yesser did not readily identify culturally with his students, whose culture and ways of interacting differed substantively from his previous experiences with other Arab populations from the Middle East. He and other teachers in the bilingual program had to maintain a precarious balance as professionals and as representatives of the Arab American community. In many ways, the teachers and their students were isolated from others in the building because the bilingual program and classes were situated in one part of the building, away from the "mainstream" and their Yemeni American peers.

Because the newcomers worked jobs with long hours for the remittances they would send home and for money to support themselves, they did not participate in after-school activities; thus they had few opportunities to interact with the other students. All the teachers at Cobb High were aware and understood that the Yemeni boys attended school only for the diploma and worked around the clock to support themselves and their families; yet tensions were not eased by this knowledge, as Mrs. Ali pointed out. Her roles as caretaker and teacher sometimes collided because she could not engage her students in high school social and academic life. For example, another Arab American teacher, Mrs. Fahzel, who taught mainly boys in the bilingual program, remarked, "Mainly, the student population that I have here, for the most part does not come specifically to learn. First of all their main purpose in coming, their main goal is to work and, and by the way, or on the wayside, along the way, they earn a degree which is also prestigious for them to take home." In other words, gaining access to a high school diploma would make for a better life in Yemen.

The tensions teachers experienced at Cobb High as the number of students of Yemeni descent increased is multifaceted. Although I did not focus in my research specifically on the lives of Yemeni newcomers but on Yemeni Americans, the newcomers were an important part of school life. Furthermore, the segregation of the bilingual program in a separate section of the high school building helps to explain the spatial and language divide among the Arab American and non-Arab teachers. These two groups of teachers did not eat lunch together or intermingle at staff meetings. They self-segregated, and this was due in part to the fact that the bilingual program was located in one section of the building, away from other subject matter classrooms. The second reason for this self-segregation is that the Arab American teachers were mostly of Lebanese descent and enjoyed eating together, sharing homemade food, and speaking a mixture of Arabic and English. Finally, these teachers were simply not comfortable with the other teachers. Mr. Ackerman, a non-Arab teacher, commented that although he ate lunch with his

(Arab) colleagues "upstairs, some of them will say they don't want to come down here because they feel they're not welcome." Some Arab American teachers contended that teachers at Cobb High were prejudiced and "could do a better job of acknowledging Islam" (interview with Mr. Jaber). Although there existed an obvious and explicit social divide among the Arab and non-Arab teachers, which included the way in which Arab American teachers related to their students, it was also true that all teachers were concerned with improving academic and social achievement for their students.

Faculty Accommodations

Accommodation at Cobb High involved the logistical and culturo-religious. Perhaps one of the most startling examples of both is the degree to which administrators respected the *hijabat*'s corporeal space. For example, at the Underclass Honors Assembly, during which 197 students received awards, 54 were Arab, and among those, 41 were Yemeni American—15 Yemeni American girls received an award for having high grade-point averages. The *hijabat* sat in a cluster at the front of the cafeteria during the ceremony while the Arab American boys sat together in the back, and everyone else, including parents, sat in mixed gender groups throughout the cafeteria. It was immediately noticeable that, as the first of the *hijabat* walked forward to the principals, she began to extend her hand and then noticed that the principals put their hands over their hearts and made a slight bow before giving her the award pin. As the rest of the *hijabat* followed suit, they all understood that they were not expected to shake their principals' hands. It turned out that a few of the *hijabat*, Saba among them, had complained in the past that having to shake a man's hand, even if he is the principal, did not show respect toward them as pious Muslims (see Chapter 4 for an example during the *Muhathara* meetings). As a result, on all public occasions, including the graduation ceremony, the principals would send a letter to the *hijabat*'s homes warning that they would be extending their hands at the event, and that if the girls did not want to make contact, they would have to wear gloves. On this particular occasion, the principals had not sent notification early enough to the girls, so they accommodated the situation by a hand to the heart and a bow.[11] This example shows the extent to which the school would accommodate its students, even when administrators forgot to send letters home. However, teachers still grappled with gender bifurcation in their classrooms and religious and cultural accommodation.

The two most significant tensions teachers faced at Cobb High were the self-segregation of the *hijabat* and the Friday afternoon leave for prayer. Teachers reacted to the *hijabat* in different ways. During the two years of fieldwork, every single teacher with whom I spoke remarked on the *hijabat*'s good study habits. According to the teachers, the *hijabat* were far more diligent about their schoolwork than any of the other students in the school. While the teachers admired the girls for their hard work, they were frustrated and confused over what they perceived to be family versus cultural issues. One English teacher, Mr. Sajek, commented that "a lot of teachers at Cobb are trying to get a feel for what's cultural and what's coming from the family." This had a direct impact on his teaching. "In other words, when we do art, we might have Michelangelo's David. It's a nude. And I've had three Arabic girls sitting next to each other and one will say I'm not allowed to look at this. And all three of them are Yemenis and will ask, you know, can I leave the room or put my head down and the others will look. You know, is that cultural or is that family?" It was this teacher's perception that "Arabic boys blend into the classroom," but the *hijabat* are "faced with living in two worlds." Another teacher, Mr. Laramy, who also taught English, shared Mr. Sajek's assessment. Mr. Laramy's classroom was an oasis for the *hijabat*. Cultural and religious norms were often suspended, but those norms also depended on content context, which made the suspension of norms more complex and nuanced. This complexity made classroom life less uniform for both teachers and students throughout the year. In the following example, Mr. Laramy comments enthusiastically about the *hijabat*'s lively engagement with content:

> The most ironic thing, I think, that I've done in the last year was when I was teaching *The Crucible* and I had all these Arabic girls in class. . . . They watched it here and they loved it and we read it, but I thought to myself, what must be going through their heads as they look at these girls, who because of their religion and culture were so, you know, penned up and unable to express themselves. And then here they are, in exactly the same situation, which is why sometimes when we, at least the last couple years, when we had problems in the school of any kind, they tended to be prolonged by the Arabic girls. They're the ones that wouldn't let it die and I thought to myself, maybe it's because for once they can kinda step forward and they're getting some attention and stuff.

In making connections between the *hijabat*'s lives at school and the literature they were reading in his class, Mr. Laramy was able to make some sense of his observations and the girls' demands for religious and cultural accommodation in the school. He was surprised at how vocal the girls could be with regard to change in the school and admitted that school was probably the only place where they could openly voice their concerns because the stakes were so high for them. In order to stay in school and maintain good grades, there had to be some religious and cultural accommodation. Going on a field trip, for example, could be problematic because the girls refused to be seen sitting in a car with their teacher and/or boys on the way to a museum. Or, as in the case of Mr. Sajek, who knew that his students could not get the help they needed at home for their homework, he was frustrated by the fact that the *hijabat* asked for help but were not allowed in his room alone after school. What was most frustrating for the teachers is that the *hijabat* were good if not exemplary students, yet they could not participate in school activities or even in some discussions on literature and other content matter, thus making classroom life complicated for their teachers. In the following passage, Mr. Sajek describes this situation as he attempted to think about what being a student entailed:

> Your heart goes out in a way to the female students because I have heard conversations and I've had conversations in the classroom where it's been indicated we wish, we wish we could do some of these things. You know, attend after-school activities. And I don't mean dances, but, you know, take part in more activities at school. I've had girls in my classroom who have broken down and cried because, you know, dealing with literature you deal with the concept of love, falling in love on your own. Whereas you know, and I've had students say, you know, I don't want someone to pick the person that I'm going to marry but I have to. . . . Your heart goes out and you see the pain of your students. It's not all of them, some are very happy.

Teachers were troubled by the fact that their Arab population did not participate in after-school activities. Because of its size, with more than 1,400 students, Cobb High was expected to compete in Division I Class A sports and other extra-curricular activities, but this was almost impossible when more than 30 percent of the school population did not participate. Teachers attempted to engage their students in school activities, in getting the necessary help after school, and in working in mixed ethnic and gender groups, but these attempts usually resulted in failure because the students refused. Teachers then let their students work in a manner that was most comfortable to them, regardless of school mandates, because they could not control the likely consequences of those mandates. For example, Mr. Sajek explained, "I have a female student who, the most recent one was a few weeks back where she's a great student but her uncle came from Yemen and when he heard that she was going to a school with boys, they're sending her back to Yemen. You know, and this teacher was broken hearted." Teachers never knew when they might lose a student because of Yemeni cultural norms, so they treaded lightly, and some, especially the five that the *hijabat* thought cared about them, learned as much as they could during interactions with their students, although the *hijabat* were often not forthcoming about cultural or religious issues.

Most teachers were frequently frustrated with accommodation

because it entailed giving up their own cultural norms—changing the cafeteria food to include humus and beef instead of pork or pepperoni or not posting any kinds of religious symbols or words on building walls during the traditional winter holidays. In fact, teachers also contended with moving the spring holiday (or Easter) to include El Eid during Ramadan, and this caused them to have a different holiday than their children, who attended other schools in the Dearborn school district. Although the teachers grumbled about these accommodations, they did acknowledge that because they had to bus the Yemenis so far from home, "it [was] only fair to recognize them and their cultural and religious practices." However, there were teachers who were angry and expressed themselves openly in their anger. Many resented the Yemeni and Yemeni American boys. As the vignette at the beginning of this chapter shows, the boys were always trying to negotiate the system. Mr. Seely, a math teacher, noted, "I get some Arabic boys that always want to negotiate their grade. That's what they're interested in. And I tell them this is not a negotiation process. This is what you earned." Mr. Laramy, who admitted that he was sexist, said that he did not expect much from the boys, but

We accommodate them grade wise. We have a number of Arabic students [boys] who pass who shouldn't. . . . We've lowered the bar educationally. . . . But you go down to the counseling office, the first two weeks after the semester starts, 90 percent of the students who were there were Arabic. Most of those students want to get changed out of a class because they didn't get the teacher they wanted, because they think it's gonna be too hard, or they want to be moved in with their friends who are in another class. And I would have to say most of these accommodations are made for them. And once the word gets out, oh, you can just go down and get out of this class and go over here where you are . . . then it becomes wholesale and it causes all kinds of problems early for the teachers particularly. The fact that an Arabic girl sometimes doesn't understand the assignment won't stop her from doing thirty pages on it. . . . The boys, on the other hand, don't, cheating is just second nature to them for the most part. It's a situation we have to deal with.

The lines that formed outside of the counselors' offices at the beginning of each semester did include mostly Yemeni students, and more often than not, the *hijabat* did not want to be in classes by themselves, so they switched to be with others like them. Overall, the teachers respected the *hijabat* for their diligence and good grades. Concerning the Yemeni and Yemeni American boys, the teachers took a more critical and sometimes hostile view. Mr. Laramy exclaimed once that he "never felt so totally helpless in all [his] life" as when he found out that one of his best female students was going to drop out of school because of a bad grade, while the boys could continue school with really low grades.

He understood that getting good grades allowed the *hijabat* to stay in school, but the fact of the matter remained that for him the accommodation process went too far if teachers had to give students good grades to keep them in school.

Other school personnel complained about the boys, especially in the cafeteria. One Lebanese American staff member, Mr. Yasseen remarked, "To be blunt, they're not civilized here. At the other high school, they're third and fourth generation. Here they're fresh, new. If you tell them, ok, you're suspended for three days, they say, c'mon, give me *one*. If you tell them, here you have a C, they'll tell you, c'mon, give me an A. They have no respect for anything. They're always negotiating and not learning how things work." Mr. Dodge, who taught science, stood out among the teachers in his comments regarding the Yemeni and Yemeni American students in the school, describing them as "a fundamental, uneducated, ignorant group." He said, "If you treat them like dogs, they're fine." In addition, the principal's policy of integration in the classroom is part of "a pretty world and we don't live in a pretty world." In describing the *hijabat*, Mr. Dodge noted that "their direction is simply breeding" and that "[they] have a difficult time at being successful because of their appearance." Finally, Mr. Dodge commented, "we get edgy with difference. It's like hanging out with retarded people. We don't want to be like them." These types of comments from a teacher elicited angry responses from students, who did complain to the administration about prejudiced teachers, and from Arab American teachers, one of whom stated, "Some teachers, they have to have more acceptance. And some, what you call, they call them white trash, they should be, they should be white, not trash."

Whereas some teachers were openly prejudiced and hostile, others simply struggled to understand and to accommodate the situation. Gym class is a prime example. Cobb High had made some formal curricular changes so that the *hijabat* could fulfill their physical education requirement without worrying about the presence of boys in the class. Unfortunately, when the changes were first instituted, a male teacher was inadvertently assigned to an all-female class, thus causing uproar. Eventually, the school ensured that these classes would be taught by women instructors, and swimming would also be taught separately to boys and girls. Nonetheless, the gym teachers were extremely frustrated by their students' behavior, as Ms. Soretsky's comments suggest:

I try to learn from them and I try to allow room for their differences. I let them wear whatever they want. So some are totally covered. But some boys walked by and they want to stop running. Well, my first instinct is no, you don't stop running. And I knew it was one of those where I might as well just adjust a little bit and two girls were very concerned about it. I let them pause and I said, ok, you owe me a minute. . . . I know that many of them have said we are not allowed to, to do anything physical in front of guys. I had to struggle a little bit. Do I push them, do I just let it go? And I'm not sure why the concern has heightened to the extent that it is but they were late for class several days in a row and I'm like, you guys, what are you doing? You can't be late. They said, well, there were guys in the hall. We didn't wanta walk across the hallway. You know, now we're getting to such extremes. I want to be considerate of the differences, I wanta be as helpful and, but I can't, I can't get to the point where kids can be tardy because they won't walk across the hallway when they're clothed any way they wanta be clothed.

Ms. Soretsky was at her wits' end. Her attempts to implement her curriculum and engage her students in class remained unsuccessful. She had difficulty understanding that the girls would rather be late to class than walk by the boys in the hallway, even when the *hijabat* were completely covered. She could not assign homework assignments to her students, such as running during the weekends, because the girls laughed and told her that they were not allowed to run. She wondered about their home life, "I think they're in two different worlds and I would be curious how in tune to this the parents are. And how many internal struggles these girls have, particularly the girls, that there's no one there to help them with." Ms. Soretsky also commented that she had heard "many teachers say I'm moving out of Dearborn because it's basically being overtaken with the Arab population. Growing up in Dearborn, especially Mayor H years and years ago, when I was a kid, it was so much Dearborn being the racist, all White community. No African Americans allowed. It's kind of funny how it's changed and stayed the same." This teacher questioned her own receptiveness toward the Yemeni in her classes. But she also worried about the girls who failed the course again and again because they did not dress appropriately (even when she allowed them to cover completely), and instead of taking three semesters of gym, they enrolled in the course for four years, and then she had to give them a passing grade (another accommodation) so that they could graduate.

The most interesting yet subtle accommodation school counselors made was to encourage the *hijabat* to enroll in family life education courses, which included foods classes, parenting, career success, interior design, and sewing. As one of the life education teachers, Mrs. Barnabey, noted:

Over the years, because the mere numbers of Arabic children in this school has grown, I have seen a larger number of Arabic students, both boys and girls. More girls than boys in my classes. I think . . . for two reasons. Number one, because the lower-ability students, not only Arabic, but Arabic and non-Arabic children alike, are encouraged to take these classes where they might have success because it's more hands on. And secondly, I think that counselors encourage the Arabic girls to take it because many of them are going to be homemakers. And thirdly, I have a lot of repeats. I have a good relationship with them and they sign up again.

At their discretion, counselors intervened in curricular decisions based on individual students' needs. One counselor commented, "The girls are basically the same as their mothers. They follow their mother's upbringing. And being home right after school, they're basically doing the same thing as the mother." This was not an accurate depiction of the *hijabat*; all of them, unlike their mothers, were literate in Arabic and English and far more educated. But early marriages and pregnancies and pressure from parents to be competent as homemakers convinced teachers and counselors that the family education classes were valuable assets for the girls. All of the *hijabat* I knew, for instance, took one or more of the family life education courses, and two enrolled in sewing because their parents told them they would need those skills in Yemen. Layla and Aisha, for instance, learned to sew just in case they moved back to Yemen and needed to make clothes for themselves and their families. In effect, the high school counselors and some teachers supported the development of competencies that they thought the girls would need once they left high school.

The counselors had much more interaction with the Arab community than did the teachers. When problems arose, they were careful not to refer potentially serious cases to the health clinic in the Southend's community center because of the likelihood of breach of confidentiality within such a tightly knit community. Also they knew that the students might be sent back to Yemen, so they protected them as much as possible unless there was no alternative. On the other hand, the counselors did utilize the community center as a resource, especially in the bilingual program, where the students participated in workshops on drugs (especially for those students who chewed *qat*) and alcohol. Importantly, the counselors facilitated parent meetings with the school. For example, because many parents were poor and could not drive the distance to school or work at night, one of the counselors had an Open House in the elementary school located in the Southend. This provided a means for parents to communicate with school personnel.

Other than the gender bifurcation issues that had troubled and frustrated teachers, the most controversial issues revolved around the inclusion of more academic content on Arab cultures and Friday prayer.[12] As to the first issue, Cobb High School's action plan as described earlier called for an increased emphasis on Arab and Islamic cultures as part of the curriculum. This confused teachers because the purpose of the increased emphasis was not clear to them. As one English teacher, Mr.

Zanak, was quick to point out, none of the students was "literate in his or her own culture," so an increased emphasis did not serve any purpose. As he put it:

> You know, people talk about cultural literacy. That's one of our, that's one of the things you hear a lot about, especially when you've got a diverse culture or a diverse population like this and people say, well, you have to do, you know, teach more about the Arabic culture to the other kids and this is something we've heard before. And you know, one of the arguments against that is, look, these kids aren't literate in their own culture. Arabic kids aren't literate in their own culture. White kids aren't literate in their own culture. It's, you know, it's a level of literacy across the board. And they don't know their history. They don't know where they came from. They don't know what was written by anybody in either culture. And yeah, that's one of our, you know, we have the humanities programs. I'm a big advocate of that because you know, we're, we're teaching art, music, and literature rolled together. And at some point, I think you arrive at a level of cultural literacy there.[13]

Another teacher insisted on focusing more on American culture because he thought an increased emphasis on Arab culture would not be as useful for the school's Yemeni population. According to him:

> I don't know if secluded is the right word, but they have asked us to instill or keep part of the Arab culture. And, in world history, that's very simple because we did that anyhow. But the one thing, this is purely opinion. This is opinion. I honestly think that many of the Yemeni, when they come here, they always seem to tell me that they're going back to Yemen and that's the reason for us, asking us to teach some of the Arab culture. And I suspect many of them will not be going back to Yemen. I suspect many of them might think they're going back but they really will stay here. And that's one reason why I also teach the American culture. Now, maybe that's prejudice on my part, thinking that American culture is a culture that's going to keep them here.

These teachers' comments indicate a willingness to overlook the action plan's objective of emphasizing Middle Eastern and Arab cultures. Such an emphasis was not for the purpose of educating the Yemeni about their own cultural and historical background in world history, although this could have been a by-product of the curriculum. The plan suggests a more deliberate approach to Arab cultures and civilizations in order to enlighten *all* students for the purpose of common understanding between Arabs and non-Arabs and for building a sense of common community membership. This was one strategy, among the many outlined in the action plan, to bridge the cultural and religious gap among students and staff. Most teachers missed this point entirely in their responses to this particular accommodation as it was laid out in the plan because they understood the accommodation process to be one-sided, an accommodation for the Yemeni population in the school.

They did not take the view that non-Arab students could benefit from changes in the social studies curriculum and that this might ease tensions among all students. In other words, if there was a deficit in knowledge, it existed among the Yemeni students rather than among non-Arab students. This view is narrow in scope because, logistically, not only does the curriculum reform fail to accommodate the growing immigrant population but it also fails to include the equally important non-immigrant population.

Accommodating Friday Prayer

One issue that drew much resentment from all teachers, Arab American and non-Arab alike, was the policy of student absence for religious reasons. On Fridays, during fifth and sixth hours, Muslim students were allowed to leave school to attend Friday prayer at the mosque. More than any other districtwide policy, this one angered teachers and some community members. In the fall of 1996, the Dearborn School District made a decision regarding the release of students on Fridays for religious instruction. Many Muslim students, mostly boys, had requested release time for Friday, the Muslim holiday, each week. Following a consultation with the school attorney, the superintendent sent a memorandum stating that a parent's request to release a student for religious instruction for up to two hours per week must be accommodated. These absences would not be penalized.[14] Between the fall of 1996 and 1998, students took advantage of this privilege and as many as fifty boys would leave school on Fridays, and not necessarily to attend religious services at the mosque. Girls generally did not leave the grounds because they had no way of getting to the mosque, while the boys could share rides among themselves. In fact, the girls said that they could pray on their own or go to the mosque after school. Their religious identities were not dependent on the mosque as a physical space because women in the Southend often prayed at home while the men prayed at the mosque.

In the fall of 1998, when Cobb High hired a community and school liaison staff member, the Friday release policy changed. The liaison staff member held a meeting in the Southend for parents who wanted their children to attend Friday mosque during the school day. Parents were invited to attend and sign their names, thus giving their permission for their children's release from school. The school received approximately twenty-four signatures, and from then on, these boys went to the mosque where attendance was taken by one of the more responsible boys under the liaison staff member's supervision. Although this school-related release improved under the leadership of the school-community liaison, teachers were still irritated that the students could leave during the school day. It came to their attention that within Islam, it was not necessary for the boys to pray between noon and two-twenty in the afternoon, that they could just as easily pray after or before school on Fridays. Teachers characterized this accommodation as "bending over backwards." Some questioned the constitutionality of the release, but as long as religious practice did not take place on school grounds, the state of Michigan and the Board of Education of Dearborn Public Schools allowed two hours of religious instruction a week. The following comment from Mrs. Barnabey is representative of the teachers' reactions to the Friday religious release. She thought that the community and religious leaders should stress attendance in school rather than religious practice during school hours.

See, well, I'm tolerant and I celebrate all religions, I truly do. But I think that we have gotten, well, let me back up. I have talked to some Muslim teachers at this school and they said nowhere in the Koran does it say that you have to stop on Friday, between noon and one to pray. That can be made up. This is relatively new. Again, I personally feel that it would be more beneficial because I feel a child's primary responsibility now is to get an education. That, but so when you miss fifth and sixth hours every single Friday, you are missing one fifth. To be honest, I do know that our school is particularly sensitive to the Arabic issue. And it seems that most of the things that are asked for are accommodated. The girls' gym class. The boys being off on Friday. Instead of saying, you know, we understand this and we appreciate this but the facts are that the Imam [Muslim religious leader] should have said education first. We pray to God later in the day. God would want you to be in school. To me, that would be, but again, you know, maybe the Imam is coming from his point of view, where he feels it is more important for them to be there. So they have to get a written permission and they do that. It's a bone of contention, I will tell you, as you can imagine.

In her comments Mrs. Barnabey listed some of the ways in which the high school accommodated the "Arabic issue," and it is clear that, to her, Friday leave was a step in the wrong direction. The Friday release for religious purposes continued to be a controversial issue, but under the supervision of the new school-community liaison staff member, it was no longer abused.[15] The school also decided that if and when other students requested a leave for holidays or religious instruction, as one Jewish girl did, they would be excused without any penalty (interview with Mrs. Jakowsky). The district worried, however, that if too many students left on any one day, they could lose substantial state funding for that day.

Accommodating Dress

It is important to note that Cobb High School accommodated its Arab students in one other significant way by letting them dress as they pleased. As I mentioned in Chapter 1, this is markedly different from policy decisions made in France not to let students wear the scarf or other religious symbols in public schools. In a memorandum from the principal to the teachers in January 1997, the principal reinforced the school's openness to dress for religious reasons with some strict guidelines:

> Just before the holiday recess, I was approached by a Muslim male student who asked if he could wear a "kuffia" which is a religious hat-like structure. I gave him permission, providing (as with our female students wearing scarves) he will never be seen not wearing his kuffia. My reason for this is that we do not allow students to wear hats in school and if a kuffia is being worn in a similar fashion as a hat, then it falls under this rule structure. I explained that should he be caught not wearing his kuffia, he would be disciplined for insubordination. He assured me that this would not happen since this was a religious decision he had made and would not be without his kuffia.
>
> This past week, I have noticed two or three other male students wearing kuffias. My intention is to treat them the same as the student mentioned above. However, I am not in a position to track these students throughout the day. Therefore, I am asking your assistance in my being consistent with this situation.
>
> If a male student is wearing a kuffia in your class, please *do not* ask him to take it off. Instead, ask to see him in private and show him this memo (or explain my position in private). Then keep a daily watch on this student to make sure he continues to wear it. If on any future day he does not wear his kuffia, please refer him to me directly (via referral) for *insubordination*. I will personally handle the situation.
>
> Your cooperation with the content of this memo will be greatly appreciated.
>
> *Note:* Some students wear the kuffia into and out of school in a similar fashion as a hat. This is not the same as wearing it throughout the school day and should be treated the same as any student wearing a hat in and out of school.[16]

Unlike the *hijabat*, the boys rarely wore religious or cultural dress at school. They all wore Western dress, whereas the girls were rarely seen without their scarves. Many of the women teachers found this differentiation in dress exasperating and often commented that it was interesting that the boys outwardly seemed to embrace Western values by wearing the latest fashions, whereas the girls had to maintain their reserved and conservative appearances. Mrs. Soretsky, one of the gym teachers, said that this was unfair and that religious dress contributed to the *hijabat*'s separateness and lack of participation in various activities. Dress did indeed prohibit the *hijabat* from participating in most activities and reinforced their identities as "good" Muslim girls within the school. This was an image the *hijabat* wanted to sustain in order to navigate successfully among home and school worlds. By accommodating their dress and the *hijab* and by being sensitive to this issue, the school administration inadvertently also helped reinforce the *hijabat*'s identities as religiously and culturally different and therefore separate from the rest of the student body.

In my examination of school archival primary sources, I found that the process through which the high school adapted to its growing population of Yemeni and Yemeni American students was complex and that both teachers and administrators faced challenging issues and charges from their communities and students. There was a range of responses from teachers, from descriptions of heartbreaking experiences to confusion to open hostility when they thought the administration has gone too far to ignorance of cultural and ethnic differences. The teachers understood their students' precarious balance in "two worlds," but they wanted some limits imposed. Most teachers were disturbed by the Yemeni students' imposed gender segregation and the self-segregation of the Yemeni community. As one teacher put it, "They just don't buy into being an American." This was troublesome for the small group of teachers who made great efforts to be accommodating and to give their students opportunities to succeed academically, only to find their hopes (and those of their students) dashed to the ground. Yet at the same time, as a school, Cobb High made some strides in the late 1990s to diversify its approach toward its population of students of diverse background and to welcome and improve educational opportunities for all.

It became clear that it would be beneficial to educators to learn more about the communities whose students they teach and to find opportunities to have discussions with the students and their parents about participation in school activities and the relationship between subject matter content and the students' cultures. As Apple (1993) has remarked, "The curriculum is never simply a neutral assemblage of knowledge, somehow appearing in the texts and classrooms of a nation. It is always part of a selective tradition, someone's selection, some group's vision of legitimate knowledge. The decision to define some groups' knowledge as the most legitimate, as official knowledge, while other groups' knowledge hardly sees the light of day, says something extremely important about who has power in society" (266).

Accommodation certainly means questioning whose knowledge is privileged and why this is so. For example, Cobb High School might diversify its faculty by assigning its Arab American teachers "mainstream" classes rather than only classes in the bilingual program. More open and informal conversations should occur among faculty around accommodation in both formal and informal curricula. Importantly, teachers need to be aware of the heavy responsibilities the *hijabat* bear as they negotiate their complicated domestic lives within their community and their social lives within the high school. The process of accommodation and understanding is by no means over, and questions linger among teachers about the secularity of the strategies used in the last several years. The school took a step in the right direction in hiring a community-school liaison staff member who would be able engage the school and community in productive conversation and action. As it turns out, there was a similar staff member position at Finkle High School, the school with approximately 75 percent of its students who were of Lebanese descent, for years. Only by giving the accommodation process more time, by comparing itself to other schools and districts in similar situations, and by continuing to involve parents and the community in its reform for cultural understanding will Cobb High School be able to judge the fruition of its efforts.

Chapter 6

From Aspiration to Desperation and Living in Ambiguity

I'm not going to be nothing when I grow up. I'm a yum-yums. I'm going to be a housewife.

—From conversation with one of the *hijabat* at Cobb High

Like when I was young, a lot, I would like always, I always like would play with my cousins. I always would be a teacher. But as they years pass by, you know. I was thinking of the easy way out, if I could ever continue my education. You know, if [I] were to be able to go to college, how long does it take to be a nurse and how long does it take to be a doctor? A teacher? I'm really concerned right now with my education. It's easier to be a teacher or nurse."

—Interview with Aisha

During my two years of fieldwork in Dearborn, it became clear that as the *hijabat* grew older, they perceived their futures as increasingly bleak and uneventful, no matter how successful they were academically or in maintaining their cultural and religious norms. All of the high school girls I shadowed—Nadya, Nouria, Saba, Amani, Aisha, and Layla—regarded their futures with trepidation, uncertain if they would be able to realize their dreams and goals. The *hijabat* intended to become nurses or teachers, occupations that met the expectations of the community and even their school. Yet for most of them developing professional careers was not likely to occur, and they therefore looked to graduation with trepidation. The intersection of public school and home expectations for success was a turbulent space for the *hijabat.* As they successfully negotiated the academic and social expectations at each grade level, they also had to attend to their community and parental expectations for success, and these sets of expectations did not complement one another. As a result, the girls' dispositions toward school, their families, and themselves became more and more negative as they approached graduation. The *hijabat's* desperation was heightened by their realiza-

TABLE 2: CLASS OF 2000 MEAN GPAs

	Female	Male	Arab Females	Non-Arab Females	Non-Arab Males	Arab Males
Fall 1997	2.713 N = 145	2.301 N = 196	2.694 N = 30	2.718 N = 115	2.357 N = 129	2.195 N = 67
Spring 1998	2.702 N = 146	2.286 N = 189	2.756 N = 31	2.688 N = 115	2.340 N = 123	2.187 N = 66
Spring 1999	2.855 N = 130	2.495 N = 155	2.957 N = 26	2.829 N = 104	2.537 N = 107	2.401 N = 48

(N = total number of students)

tion that they had little say in the decisions made about their futures. They lived their last two years of high school in ambiguity, for they did not know whether they would be sent to Yemen to marry or finish high school and even be allowed to pursue careers. Although the *hijabat* become quite desperate about their status as Yemeni women in their American world, they maintained their grade-point averages in the hope of continuing their education after high school. Doing well in school, no matter what their futures had in store for them, allowed them to hope.

The All-Important GPA

As ninth graders the *hijabat* had strong aspirations for their futures. They saw themselves graduating from high school and then attending college. By the time they reached the twelfth grade, however, they were desperate to stay in school and maintain a high GPA. They compared their lives to those back home, in Yemen. Layla, from the class of 2000, commented, "If you live in Yemen, you get married because there's nothing else to do. Here you can do things with your life." Knowing that obtaining an education might give them opportunities they would not have elsewhere, the *hijabat* worked very hard at school in order to be able to stay and perhaps continue their education. Table 2 shows the grade-point averages over two years for the class of 2000 at Cobb High School.

The mean grade points of all the high school girls were higher than those of the boys.[1] By the spring of 1999, the Arab girls' GPAs were higher than those of the non-Arab girls.[2] The class of 1999 had a similar distribution although the non-Arab girls were slightly ahead in the spring of 1999 with a mean grade point of 2.972, whereas the Arab girls had a mean grade point of 2.840. The classes of 2001, 1998, and 1997 also showed a distribution where the non-Arab girls were slightly ahead of the Arab girls. Overall, the boys' GPAs were lower than those of the girls, and the Arab boys' GPAs were lower than those of the non-Arab boys.[3]

The Arab American girls' (most of whom were of Yemeni origin) relatively high GPAs are the result of several factors. The fact that the *hijabat* did not work outside the home and did not participate in after-school activities and sports ensured that they had more than enough time to complete their schoolwork. Teachers often described the *hijabat* as diligent students who handed in work either on or ahead of time. Second, being a good female student in the Yemeni community was equated with being a "good girl," one who upholds the family honor. Third, doing well in school meant having a possible ticket to a career outside the home and community. Unlike the Yemeni boys, for whom high school meant getting a credential (diploma), getting by with a passing grade was not enough for the *hijabat*—they were not allowed to work outside the home and/or community after high school. But having the opportunity for more education was still a viable option, especially if scholarships were available for college. For example, both Sabrina and Mariam were able to attend nearby universities because they were awarded scholarships. In Sabrina's case, her father negotiated that she would be allowed to finish college as part of the marriage agreement with her Yemeni husband. In Mariam's case, her older brother attended college and this enabled her to go. Both of these young women, unlike most of the *hijabat* at the time, were able to continue their education because they had excellent grades while in high school and because in their cases, the men in their families supported this decision.

Teachers at Cobb High did notice the *hijabat*'s preoccupation with grades. For example, Mr. Ackerman, one of the social studies teachers, remarked that he did not understand their obsession with grades: "I don't see them going on to school once they leave here because my perception is that these Muslim girls don't go on to higher education. You rarely hear them speak about what they're going to do." Mr. Ackerman described one of the *hijabat* in his advanced placement history class:

I know these girls are studying very hard. I know that each of them is keeping track, every time I pass a paper back, they get a little grid out and they write everything down to keep track of where they are and if something comes back, and they get like a calculator out to try to figure. And I've tried to say to them, you know, don't do that because they, I'm trying to get across to them that different grades mean different things in terms of like . . . cuz the multiple choice tests will be 1/3 of the grade, essays are 1/3, notebooks are 1/3, and they're just looking at oh, my gosh, I got a bad score here. I'm not doing well. And I say, you know, you can't do that. You've got to wait until the end of the marking period, look at it overall, and if a grade here seems low, you gotta remember that this is coming in later and that most likely will boost the grade because of what it's going to be, this type of thing. And I've had to do that several times to try to reassure them that they're, that they're doing better than what they think they are. I got this sense for this girl that there was, there was pressure from home to have a higher GPA. I got that sense. Because she mentioned her dad a couple of times, you know.

The *hijabat* experienced much self- and parental pressure regarding grades. Layla's mother, for instance, told me that she pushed her daughter to get good grades; otherwise there was no point of letting her stay in school. She also thought that teachers were "too easy" on her daughter and should make her work harder. Nouria's mother was perplexed by her daughter's lower grades in comparison to those of her older daughters and told her to write as much as possible. Mr. Ackerman was one of several teachers who observed that if they could not maintain a high grade point average, the girls were likely to drop the class. It is important to note, too, that although the *hijabat*'s fathers made final decisions about marriage, mothers were also a strong influence with regard to school and grades. Layla's mother, for instance, bemoaned her daughter's less-than-perfect GPA. Aisha's mother, on the other hand, preferred to see her daughter married and out of school, so Aisha was under constant pressure from both parents and had to maintain her 4.0 average every semester—she put pressure on herself because if she faltered even slightly, she would have to drop out and get married. At one point she confided, "I'm like in a bad position because my father wants to marry me in like one year and forever. I'm gonna be a senior and they want to leave [to go back to Yemen]. And that just, I've been so depressed about that." Her school counselor, Mr. Vestsy, commented that he "push[ed] the girls' families to let their daughters take the PSAT by telling them that their kids could possibly go to college for free." He persuaded Aisha to let her family know that she could get a scholarship once he noticed how depressed she was about the possibility of not being able to finish school and not going to college. Aisha, like most of the *hijabat*, was willing to be a teacher or nurse because any other career path would take too long and would try the patience of her parents, but the notion of attending college remained a question in her life.

The Power of the Curse

It is clear that the *hijabat*'s success at school—having a high GPA and behaving according to Yemeni cultural and religious norms—was intimately connected with their status as "good daughters" at home and in their community. Being successful at school meant that the *hijabat* spent their time wisely by studying at home and being helpful with housekeeping, thus doing little else that would elicit questions from their families and community. There were times, though, when the *hijabat* openly disagreed with their parents' decisions, and the consequences could be harsh. Other than being forced to marry, the *hijabat* feared the curses their families would throw at them. During my two years in Dearborn, it was apparent that curses were a taboo topic and that the curses rested on an underlying belief system that parallels that of Islam. One of the women who worked in the community, for example, told me that the Yemeni believe in good and evil spirits and that when one of the *hijabat* was sent to Yemen for misbehaving, she would come back a different person—with physical (and sometimes mental) symptoms of having been cursed. These curses, according to community members, would be said while the intended person ate something, which could be drugged to produce the desired effect, such as a rash or a stupor. For example, the high school *hijabat* often warned me not to drink tea served by the old women in the Southend or in Yemen.

In school, the belief in curses manifested itself in interesting ways. Saba, the girl who wanted to marry someone of her own choosing, spent a week in the hospital after an altercation with her mother in the Southend and her uncles in Yemen. Her family refused to acknowledge the man she had chosen. Upon her return to school, Saba stated that she feared her family's curses, which had sent her into a fit of depression in the first place. Several of the *hijabat* in the community commented that the curses could affect their GPAs, so they had to be careful about everything and make sure that the boaters never looked them in the eye.[4] Those *hijabat* who worried about curses or evil spirits recited the Ayat El Kursi and the Surat El Baqara from the Qur'an each night in order to ward them off.

Negotiating home and school expectations within the Southend was no easy feat for the *hijabat*. Maintaining a good GPA, constantly performing within cultural and religious boundaries at school, cooking and cleaning and looking after siblings, managing the household finances, coping with husbands' housekeeping and personal demands (if married), pregnancy, avoiding marriage as long as possible, and being careful not to incite any curses—these practices defined the *hijabat*'s lives while in high school. By fulfilling all of these duties well, the *hijabat* had the chance to realize the futures they envisioned.

Fatalistic and Depressed

The teachers at Cobb High School characterized the *hijabat*'s dispositions from ninth to twelfth grade as steadily more "depressed," "fatalistic," and characterized by "low morale," while most of the Yemeni boys would "barely get by and get the diploma" and left school pleased at the prospect of working and in a few cases going to college. The girls often expressed their frustration at not knowing what they would do after graduation as their families decided their futures and their teachers could only listen. The *hijabat* were never really aware of how their teachers felt or reacted to what they said. Mr. Dodge, one of the science teachers, said, "Girls' future, [as] I see . . . the girls and [the way] I've heard them speak of it, it's very fatalistic. Yemenis leave after school and go back home. To the fatalistic environment. This my fate. I will go home and I will make dinner. I will clean this. I will care, watch my brothers. You know, that's what they'll tell you too."

Like Mr. Dodge, one of the school counselors, Mr. Abdullah, pointed out that the *hijabat*'s grades might slip as their morale slipped: "Their grades are slipping, the morale slips, the enthusiasm slips. They know, even if they get a diploma, they're not going anywhere with that diploma because they're not going to college. They're gonna raise a family, a large family, and whatever the husband says goes. So, the majority of the time, even if they can get that diploma, there's no use for that diploma." Another teacher, Mrs. Barnabey, simply said, "The girls cannot dream." She reiterated that some do go on to more education, but for most, the future is a "bleak" one. One of the more poignant observations was made by one of the gym teachers, Mrs. Soretsky:

> I see dramatic change in the girls from ninth to twelfth grade. Not just the usual changes of the kids growing up. I see such a pattern of these girls getting—a lot of them seem to get depressed their senior year. A lot of them get very withdrawn. I watch their personalities change dramatically and I always thought that it was due to the fact that they would be leaving school and [for] many of them their lives will drastically change if they're not going on to college. I had one student, before she graduated, she stood and she's talking to me and she said, "You know," she said, "I look at all of these awards that are in the hallway, the athletic awards," she said, "and I would have been so good at basketball and I would have been so good at," I don't know what other sports she named. She said, "I wasn't allowed." And she said, "I will never, ever forgive my parents for that." And for her to be even open enough to say it, 'cause many, they feel they're not honoring their parents and not being appropriate by voicing something like that. But it just broke my heart, just broke my heart.

Ms. Soretsky, too, felt helpless as she listened to her Yemeni American female students. She pointed out that "there's a kind of push and pull to maintain [their] culture but yet fit in. . . . There's two different worlds." The conflict the *hijabat* faced as they dared to speak out about their desperation was prohibiting. One of the Arab American teachers, Ms. Ishmael, suggested that the *hijabat* kept everything inside because they were afraid of the consequences of speaking out:

The conflict stays inside. It's not outspoken. She'll never answer her mom, you stay out of it, you keep out of it. No, there's no such thing. She'll cry and feel depressed inside without nobody knowing it. So everything's kept to themselves. It's not out. Because if she speaks out, that means you're not raised well. You are bad. You've become a bad person. You're not following your religion. You are dada, you know, and then you are not good for the community not good for the family and if people find out about you, they're gonna think you are bad. So, it's all hush, hush, hush.

The teachers understood the *hijabat*'s reticence concerning their private struggles to deal with their futures. At the same time those teachers, who would normally have encouraged their students to take all the necessary steps to attend college, could not do so with the *hijabat* who were good students. The teachers could only remain silent when the *hijabat* expressed the dissonance of home and school worlds. This ran counter to both the school's and teachers' expectations about what should happen to their high achieving students.

Desperate and Living in Ambiguity

The six high school *hijabat* and their friends at Cobb High School expressed their desperation about the future in different ways over the two years that I spent in the community. Nouria, from the class of 2000, wanted to divorce her husband. She said, "I hate my life. I want to get the hell out of this place." Amani, from the class of 1999, said that she wished that she could remove her scarf and wear short sleeves and become a nurse or teacher. Aisha, a top student from the class of 2000, was finally happy to learn, during her eleventh-grade year, that she could finish high school, although her family arranged for her to marry and go to Yemen following her graduation. Layla, also from the class of 2000, said that she worried about her grades, which were average, especially as she was trying to avoid marriage to her first cousin from Yemen. Nadya, from the class of 2001, knew that she could go to college because her older sister was married and enrolled in college, but she did not know if she would be allowed to go because her grades were not as high as those of her sister. Saba, from the class of 1999, talked about her unwillingness to go to Yemen and marry: "I believe that victory comes with those who are patient. If I, I let it get to me, it will eat me alive. I'm being patient in the sense where I'm not, you know, committing suicide."

In contrast to the *hijabat*'s desperation about their futures, the two boys who allowed me to interview them expressed markedly different views about their futures. Fateh, from the class of 1999, said, "I can do anything I want now. I can do anything." Malek, from the class of 2000, stated, "all I want to do is finish high school and then don't worry what

I do. Whatever I do, happens. I don't know. I'm not looking for the future yet. I'm just looking to get my education and do whatever feels right for me to do." These responses from the boys were typical of the comments made informally to me by all the Yemeni American boys in the high school and illustrate that, indeed, they had a choice to pursue more than one option after they graduated, although both Fateh and Malek were expected to have good grades and to work after school. Yet, as their comments suggest, there is a lack of pessimism, depression, and fatalistic outlook, which characterizes the girls' responses.

The ambiguity with which the *hijabat* faced their futures conflicted with their school's goal of producing educated citizens who will contribute to society. As Peshkin (1986) notes, "The artistic, literary, social, and religious riches of our society, are a product of minds able to operate under relatively open conditions" (287). As long as the *hijabat* are constrained by the expectations of the Southend and Yemen, they are unlikely to benefit from or contribute to American society. Even as they express themselves in the in-between spaces of school and home discussed in Chapter 4, or even as they engage more freely in classroom life, as I noted in Chapter 3, the fact is that, as members of the Yemeni community in the Southend, for most of the *hijabat*, their lives might be cognitively and socially limited by the spaces they occupy—mostly the home and immediate neighborhood and the ever-present Yemeni village. As long as they continue to marry men from Yemen who have little or no education, they are likely to relive their parents' lives in the Southend. Of course, as one of the school counselors suggested when I talked with him, perhaps the *hijabat* will return to school once they have children. That is a possibility, but whether this will happen and whether they will become the teachers and nurses they would like to be, remains an open question.

Some broader implications can be drawn from my fieldwork in 1997–99. Perhaps the most salient one is that key concepts such as success, identity, ethnicity, and gender must be understood as shifting processes in which the dynamic enactment of culture and religion remain highly nuanced. Research on the relationship between homes, communities, and schools ought not be limited solely to the study of social class differences. Even though the *hijabat* came from low socioeconomic status homes in which the parents were predominantly print-illiterate, they still succeeded academically and maintained relatively high grade-point averages. In addition, the relationship between social class and social and cultural capital should be rethought and conceptualized in ways that take into account the very real role religion plays in community and school life. If anything, the *hijabat*'s sometimes complex, self-contradictory, and individually variable experiences illustrate the multifaceted and emergent nature of identity, self, religion, and literacy. For example, notions of success and how they are related to teenagers' views of formal education, Islam, use of language, college, delay of marriage, Yemen, and being in the United States are often contradictory. The contradictions reflect the continuation of polyvocal and conflicted discourses around schooling and education in the *hijabat*'s families, community, and teachers.

Another implication drawn from this work is that the Yemeni American immigrant relationship to Cobb High School runs counter to the common sense view of "nonmainstream" cultures and public schools in general. Previous research cited throughout the book on immigrant and minority populations in the United States, has shown that public schools historically have resisted adapting to the needs of their new nonmainstream populations and have not, in general, embraced the notion of multicultural curricula. However, Cobb High School accommodated the Yemeni and the *hijabat* in remarkable ways. The process of accommodation remains ongoing and illustrates that schools can reform both formal (academic) and informal (social) curricula in order to meet the needs of *all* students. As Apple (1993/1997) argues, this is the main aim that society holds for public schools and teachers in a democracy. The process seems to begin with a handful of teachers and community members with a vision for connection and mutual engagement in a common progressive educational endeavor. In addition, the high school proved to be the *hijabat*'s greatest source of opportunity for self-expression and openness. The openness of their high school afforded a unique space for identity development. Understanding this, the *hijabat* took an active role in shaping their environment in order to ensure that they would remain in school and therefore attempt to fulfill future aspirations.

Public school, however, was not always a uniformly liberating experience for the *hijabat* or their teachers. As soon as the accommodation process began, home and school worlds often collided. The *hijabat*'s interactive performances as students, girls, Muslims, and Yemeni American daughters, sisters, and wives were all context dependent and highly variable, and that variability in identity impacted their social and academic lives and continues to do so today. The high school itself, as an institution, remained fragmented because teachers', administrators', and parents' visions for schooling and education differed. This fragmentation was evidenced in two ways: the Arab American and non-Arab teachers held themselves responsible for their students' lives differently, thus creating a professional separateness within the building, and this often caused tension; and at times, the school actually reinforced the *hijabat*'s gendered and religious identities, which could be construed as less than liberating. In such instances, in order to avoid stereotypes and ambiguity and to encourage thoughtful responsiveness, schools, parents, students, teachers, administrators, and the communities they serve should attempt to learn more about one another and the children they teach and find ways to engage more productively across school and home settings.

Chapter 7

Living Ethnography: Reflections on Dearborn Before and After September 11

We don't know who we are anymore.
—Layla, February 2002

In 1999, I ended my fieldwork at the Olive Garden restaurant in Dearborn, in the company of Saba, Aisha, Layla, Nouria, Nadya, Sabrina, Mariam, and Mrs. Dunbar, my main contact in the Yemeni community who had introduced me to the *hijabat* and their families. We chose the Olive Garden because it was close to the girls' homes and because the girls said they had never been there nor had they had the opportunity to eat Italian American food. As we sampled the calamari, spinach dip, and various pasta dishes, the conversation ebbed and flowed around topics familiar to all of us: weddings in Yemen, Hollywood films, and school gossip. At the end of dinner, I gave each of the girls an empty journal as a gift and a pretty scarf to Mrs. Dunbar. I wrote, "They seemed to like these small gifts, and I am sad to be leaving them behind in the lives I've uncovered. It's very hard to just leave." I knew my work in the field was finished when we stopped at my apartment on the way home, and I gave my TV and some other household items to one of the newly married young women.

As I think back to that last dinner, I find it remarkable that the girls' parents allowed me to take the *hijabat* away from the Southend, however briefly. We left the smokestacks behind and feasted happily beyond the prying eyes we all knew from the community and school. A few of the *hijabat* even considered removing their scarves in the restaurant before discarding that idea. Of course, the presence of Mrs. Dunbar testified to the safety of the event, but I knew that this dinner could not have taken place a year or even two years before, when I first arrived in the field.

I remember that when I first arrived in the Southend in early 1997, I introduced myself as a researcher who wanted to learn more about what it meant to be successful at home and school for Yemeni American girls. I gained access to the community after making contact with individuals who worked in the community center in the Southend, and these key informants facilitated my initial meetings with the *hijabat* and their parents. I lived in the community while I conducted fieldwork, and my native knowledge of Arabic and my college study of Fous'ha, or literary Arabic, and general familiarity with Islam facilitated my access to the Southend, people's homes, the mosque, social gatherings, and Arabic school.

Initially, my fieldwork entailed learning about both boys' and girls' lives in the Southend, but as a woman researcher, it proved difficult for me to gain access to the male domains. The data I gathered in the girls' and women's domains is far richer and more complete than what I could gather about boys and men. My own mixed ethnic (Algerian and Greek) identity was problematic at times, as some community members, even a few of the *hijabat* in the Southend, attempted to change my non-religious stance to that of a devout and practicing Muslim. As I describe throughout the book, cultural and religious practices were often intertwined in the Yemeni community, and although I was familiar with and had read about many Islamic traditions, the particularities of Yemeni religious and cultural life were often alien to me, and I was very much an outsider in that respect.

Later, as I paged through my field notes in southern California, I found solace in the fact that other ethnographers had had similarly powerful personal experiences in the field. Duneier's (1999) appendix for *Sidewalk* is a fine example and testament to the rigor of personal and professional involvement in fieldwork and of living ethnography, and as I read his book, I too wanted to highlight what Michael Agar calls "rich points" in this kind of work. I think that this is a key component of any ethnography because it addresses the how, when, and why of the project. Importantly, although methodological appendices are currently more prevalent than they have been in the past, there are not enough of them. Annette Lareau's (2000) *Home Advantage* is still one of the most compelling and widely cited and utilized guides for students and scholars who are interested in research methodology and education. I hope this final chapter will contribute and add to this tradition of laying bare the work involved in the ethnographic process, which is rare in education studies.

As I wrote this book, there were several key events, spanning from 1997 to 2002, that I think, when viewed together in succession, lend a broader perspective to my presence in the field. These interconnected narrative events, among others, explain how one might live ethnography, especially in the aftermath September 11, 2001. The narratives are the story of writing this ethnography. They are *writing stories,* "narratives about contexts in which the writing is produced. . . . They offer critical reflexivity about the writing-self in different contexts as a valuable creative analytic practice" (Richardson 2000:931). Furthermore, this kind of narrative situates the author's writing in the author's life, which for me includes my academic work within my institution and fieldwork in immigrant communities in the months before and after the attacks of September 11. The narratives evoke questions about meaning and serve as a reminder that our work and this book are contextual and that the relationship between the social practice of "doing fieldwork" and education is a dialogical one. More than ever, I became aware that doing fieldwork in a highly politicized community is a transformative and dangerous experience for both the researcher and the informant and that public education serves as a constant democratizing agent of hope and liberation during uncertain political and economic times.

A Nonthreatening Presence

I arrived at Cobb High School right after the "cafeteria incident" (see Chapter 5) and during a time of high tension and frustration for the teachers and students. This was a coincidence, of course, although I viewed it more as an opportunity to learn something interesting. No one knew what to make of my presence, and teachers were quick to complain about me when I first began to "shadow" the students. They worried that I was there to evaluate their instruction and that I would report back to the administration about what I observed in their classrooms. However, even before that, when I was first introduced to the principal by one of the Dearborn School District directors, I remember sitting quietly in the principal's office while he and the director discussed what I would be doing. At one point the director said, "It's really a coincidence that she's here when we've had all these problems. She didn't know about them until this week. I don't think this will be a problem. She has a nonthreatening presence." The principal readily agreed to this estimation of my appearance, and I was on my way. It took a little more time to convince teachers that I was, in fact, keeping my observations notes to myself and that I was indeed nonthreatening.

Over time, I found that having a nonthreatening presence worked to my advantage in conducting fieldwork, even when I had to meet with teachers after school one day to talk one more time about what I was doing in their classrooms. I remember agreeing to sit or stand wherever they thought I should and to be as unobtrusive as possible. After that meeting, the principal told me once again that my nonthreatening presence had helped tremendously and that I could carry on.

Although I was immensely relieved to gain access to the teachers' classrooms when I shadowed students, the test to my nonthreatening presence occurred with my first interview of one of the high school *hija-bat*, Saba. A natural leader, Saba would determine the course of my relationships with all six of the focal high school *hijabat*. She knew that I was familiar with the Arab world, that I was born in Algeria and could read and write in Arabic. This had eased some of the tension before the interview. However, one of my goals was to audiotape the interviews, but this would not have been possible if Saba had not agreed to let me record her interview. I remember scratching at my interview protocol, trying to keep up with Saba's comments; I remember telling her that I was a faster typist than writer, but I hadn't thought about typing the responses to the interview; I remember looking at her in frustration as I attempted to write exactly what she said. Finally, one-third of the way through the interview, she did say, "Ok, Loukia. I trust you. I know that if you record this interview, it will be anonymous. Plus, you don't look like someone who could be threatful." I let out a whoosh of relief and turned on the tape recorder.

I was grateful to be characterized as nonthreatening. By the end of my fieldwork, my nonthreatening presence enabled me to thank the *hijabat* properly, by going out to dinner in relative privacy and by talking openly. But, living ethnography is never as simple as turning a tape recorder on or off. When I returned to Dearborn in February 2002 and shared publications based on my fieldwork, I found that September 11 had created a void between some of the young women and me. For instance, two of the *hijabat* who had been adamant about Americans knowing more about Yemeni culture and religion, expressed their anxiety regarding published text related to their marriages or struggles to avoid marriage. Even though they had agreed multiple times in the past that what I recorded could be used in articles and books, September 11 added to a growing fear of telling their personal stories so openly. This contradicted, in some ways, the fact that many of the young people in Dearborn were telling their stories to the public media, including CBS's *60 Minutes*. I had agreed, then, to modify some sections regarding marriage but to keep all of the information necessary for readers to begin to understand what it means to be one of these young women living in the United States. This experience serves as a reminder that living ethnography goes beyond the field and can be a haunting journey during the most tragic of political times.

The Quest for a Mailbox: Becoming an Insider

One of the more difficult aspects of conducting research as an outsider in a public school on a daily basis is not having a place through which one can collect information or have others leave information. During the first year of fieldwork, I did not have a way to collect daily bulletins and other materials at Cobb High unless I found the material posted on the wall, or I hunted it down in teachers' classrooms and photocopied it. I had also made photocopies of notes to teachers alerting them about a classroom visit when I shadowed one of the students but had no place to put those either. Finally, halfway through the first year, one of the secretaries agreed to keep a folder for me on her desk, and I was able to check incoming mail there. Unfortunately, teachers would never remember this folder when everyone else received mail in mailboxes specifically designed for daily mail. So, during that academic year, mail was not delivered to me—I anticipated its delivery and picked it up instead.

When I returned to school during the second academic year, much to my surprise, I was given one of the empty mailboxes alongside those of the teachers. This changed my life at Cobb High in a dramatic way. Teachers could now leave me notes or respond to inquiries. I would get a copy of the daily bulletin and other materials. More importantly, I felt as if I had finally become an insider of sorts, part of the school culture and privy to the information others were getting. It was easier for me to take note of scheduled meetings and plan around teachers' and students' schedules. My quest for a mailbox ended, and I'll be forever grateful that the secretaries in the main office finally gave me one.

The Limitations of Being a Woman at a Yemeni Funeral

One of the most heart-wrenching moments in the field was the day I attended the funeral of one of the *hijabat*'s brothers. She was one of the six I shadowed, and her younger brother died in a car accident in front of Cobb High. I remember rushing to the school to see if I could give any of the girls a ride to the mosque to attend the services and then rushing back to the mosque for the noon prayer. I worried that the scarf I hastily took out of my bag as I approached the mosque did not adequately cover my head, but when I arrived, I saw that other women, who did not usually cover their heads, had the same problem, so I just let mine slip and would pull it back when necessary. I sat in a stuffy basement room with hundreds of women from the community and the school. We listened to the voice of the Imam over the loudspeaker and prayed silently. I sat near the *hijabat*, holding the hand of one of them.

I was confused about what we were all doing in the stuffy basement room of the mosque when the body of the boy was upstairs. I was told that only the men could be with the body while the women had to remain downstairs. Finally, we were told that we could go outside and watch the procession from the mosque to the Muslim section of the large cemetery in the Southend. What I experienced outside shocked me, and it was then that I felt the limits of being a woman during this event.

We wait outside and I notice that across the parking lot, there are school buses. I walk over there and in doing so, I leave the *hijabat* behind and find myself in a sea of men and boys. They all stare, but I walk with the Lebanese American teachers. The buses are full of football players and cheerleaders bearing flowers. They're not sure what to do and they don't know that they've missed the prayer. This is their first (and perhaps only) time into the Southend.

I watch the front of the mosque. The *hijabat* do not walk where they can see what is happening, and the Lebanese American teachers tell them that it's ok to come to the front. But the girls hang back as a group and say that there are too many men. While the men walk around in the parking lot and in front of the mosque staring at the women, the *hijabat* stand in one large cluster in the back, craning their necks to see. Many are crying. Yet they stand together in a group of more than seventy-five, clustered together as the men walk past and around them, staring.

Finally, men walk out of the mosque carrying the casket. All the men (more than 300) crowd around it as they all walk to the cemetery. The women hang back and very hesitantly walk toward the cemetery. The Lebanese teachers urge them on, but even Amani doesn't go into the cemetery, and she's the sister of the dead boy. Instead, the women stand on the edge of the parking lot and look across the street into the cemetery.

In every sense, the women are outsiders in this drama of grief. They fear stepping forward and becoming part of the funeral procession, and they fear being close to the men in the cemetery. They watch while the men carry out the process. They are stared at as if they are alien. At one point, a photographer photographs them, and I see what he sees: a group of about seventy-five covered women (in black and white) standing so close together that one would have a hard time walking through. The men, on the other hand, are dispersed, in clusters of one to six men and walk wherever they please. The women's movements are dependent on that of the men. They maintain the appropriate distance.

The Lebanese women tell me that they've never been to a funeral like this one where women don't stand where they like and around the grave. They say that this is *haram* and sad. One of the teachers says that this mosque was built by the Lebanese years ago and women never had to cover themselves if they didn't want it so. "Now, everything has changed since the Yemeni population has grown and taken over."

Other outsiders include school officials and non-Arab students. They stand out as different, not Arab, and they don't understand what they should do. Their clothes are different and their stance is different. They're confused. The football players' heads are shaved, a sharp contrast to the bearded heads of the Arabs.

I can't see the casket being lowered. There are too many men around the grave. I ask some of the girls when it is that women can go to the grave. They point out to me that there are some women standing to the right side near the grave. I see a few scarfed heads, but immediately around, it is only men I see.

I still don't know how the *hijabat* dealt with their grief from the distance they had to maintain at the funeral. Their space was clearly demarcated by the positioning of the men—they feared the consequences of breaking away from their cluster and walking to the grave. They became observers in a drama of grief in which the men participated fully and the women only marginally. As one of the women present, I too took on the role of observer. I could only watch, as did the *hijabat*, keeping my own emotions under control.

Crafting Post–September 11 Selves: What Does It Mean to Be American?

As an immigrant of North African (Algerian) and European (Greek) descent and as an American living in the Midwest, I, like many others, participated in public and media discourses focused on ethnicity and religion in the aftermath of the September 11 attacks. Throughout the fall of 2001, after revising various drafts of this book and participating in those debates, I noticed that among people who use compound labels, I was perceived and categorized as either Euro American or Arab American or was regarded as a hybrid (an American). While many questioned my "unusual" name, the inevitable question arose: "So, what are you?" I wondered if there is a way to respond to the dilemma that the "what are you?" question poses in times of crisis and catastrophe and, in the wake of the attack, I became more interested in understanding how our communities adapt to the often subtle and sometimes explicit demands on our emotions, our time, and our intellect in the private and public spaces of our lives such as schools, communities, and homes. How do individuals and communities *re*-present themselves in the context of such an attack and its complex and complicated aftermath, including a new war in the Middle East?

It has long been considered a truism that how we perceive, represent, and act around others defines our individual and collective identities. The September 11, 2001, tragedy and the ensuing political and military events rendered people in the United States and elsewhere more sensitive to the particularities of perception and representation. Throughout this book and elsewhere, I have suggested that immigrant communities live in the in-between spaces created in the nexus of ethnicity, nationality, and culture, and that people's textual and social practices reflect and refract their in-betweenness (Sarroub 2002c). However, during times of crisis, people inevitably have to choose how to represent themselves, and being in-between may not satisfy local and national expectations of what it means to be a member of a given community. My own Algerianness was foreground on both personal and professional levels after September 11. For example, like most people around the world, I watched and read the news avidly, and I cringed every time I noted that yet another individual from the Middle East was part of the attack, and I was ever watchful of Algerians' possible participation in this act of terror. I watched and I too wondered if I was watched under the panoptican-like gaze.

The "what are you?" question became a haunting metaphor for the fear and apprehension I witnessed in various immigrant communities, and my work on Arab Muslim youth in the United States became more significant as I attempted to answer hundreds of questions from educators, researchers, and neighbors. People wanted to know more, for example, about where these Arab and Arab American communities are located, who the youth are in our schools, and how they might be related to the events of September 11. This process of answering questions and looking at research through the tragic lens of September 11 indexed something new in my work and that of colleagues who study a range of communities in the United States. Catastrophic events and their consequences had to be interrogated through a critical lens no matter where they occurred. Research sites were no longer just schools and/or communities that could be discreetly described and analyzed and then discussed in the research community. The geopolitical ramifications of the attack underscored the notion that everyone is an active participant, a participant observer, and deeply embedded in the consequences of such a catastrophe, especially in this digital age where images and text are so quickly and easily accessible. In effect, we all became observers of our participation as individuals across the United States and elsewhere grew more watchful or, in many cases, more watched.

Since September 11, people in the United States and much of the world have been engaged in three broad discourses: 1) war, 2) security versus civil liberties, and 3) inclusion and discrimination. For example, we have all wondered if we are at war and if fighting terrorist networks means that we are fighting a *new* kind of war. Most of us have experienced the new security measures at airports and debated the advantages and disadvantages of national identification cards. Finally, in the United States, discrimination and "racial profiling" at all social and professional levels have long and complicated histories and continue to be problematical, societal issues. I became interested in the third discourse on inclusion and discrimination in the context of my research conducted in Arab American communities and, in particular, in Dearborn, where I first learned about the *hijabat* and their families. At the heart of this discussion are the questions "Who is American, and what does it mean to be an American?" This closely relates to the "what are you?" question. Since September 11, we have observed, watched, and participated in a public accounting of this question. For example, in Gregory Rodriguez's September 23, 2001, *New York Times* article "Identify Yourself: Who's American?" the following observations were made about U.S. society:

1) Not until the 1960s was it permissible for immigrants to adhere to their cultural heritages. The definition of citizenship shifted from belief in a common culture to following shared ideals.
2) Since the 1970s multiculturalism nurtured unprecedented levels of public tolerance of ethnic and racial differences and respect for hyphenated identities.
3) Some people even espoused a form of multiculturalism that challenged the need for immigrants and other minorities to identify with America at all.
4) By the end of the twentieth century, being American simply meant being a participant in the search for wealth and stability.

The attacks of September 11 changed what seems to have been a rather flexible ideology of Americanness.[1] The attacks provoked renewed vigor and an explicit accounting of its citizenry. Individuals found ways to identify with being Americans. Many flew American flags on their cars, their lawns, and in front of their businesses. Others held vigils for the lives lost in the attacks. Most residents of the United States experienced renewed respect and awe for firefighters, police officers, and others in the business of public safety and publicly recognized their efforts. Still others played or watched football, a national pastime, or watched the awkwardness of late night comedy show hosts, who, for the first time, said that they had nothing funny to say. In some communities, many spent time explicitly and publicly defending their American identities. As I began a new fieldwork project in an Iraqi refugee community in the fall of 2001, I observed young men shaving their beards, and I read daily school bulletins in which teachers and principals encouraged understanding and tolerance, especially of Islam in the United States. Without exhausting the myriad ways people found to display their Americanness, my point is that they did, and in doing so, they had to re-present themselves because they (we) were all participants and observers of our participation as we (they) attempted to answer the "what are you?" question.

Agar (1994) discusses the concept of languaculture, that one cannot understand a language or culture without being aware of both, of their implicit and explicit connection, that in order to understand a "culture," a person has to understand himself/herself in it. This is apropos of September 11. For days following the attack, major television networks engaged us explicitly in a redefining process, one that enacted new cultural and linguistic norms that questioned and analyzed what it means to be American. As Kondo (1990) writes, "Crafting selves implies a concept of agency: that human beings create, construct, work on, and enact their identities, sometimes creatively challenging the limits of cultural constraints which constitute both what we call selves and the ways those selves can be crafted" (48). Of course, in the months and years following the attacks of September 11, what is at stake is our potential as educators, researchers, community members, and families to continue to foster sites, such as schools, classrooms, community centers, homes, work places, and the like where individuals can in fact have the opportunity to craft who they would like to be.

Being Wanded

In November 2002, en route to Washington, D.C., for an American Anthropology Association meeting, I flew to New Jersey with a connection in Minneapolis before landing at the Newark airport. While in Minneapolis during my one-hour stay, I encountered a new verb and a new noun, words in the English language that perfectly illustrate the tragic and sociolinguistic consequences of September 11. People learned to adapt and adopted linguistic forms (and neologisms) to reflect a changing set of ideas, ways of being in a cultural and socioeconomic market that was telling them to continue to engage in the usual norms of society and at the same time strive to be more alert, suspicious, and careful. In effect, they learned a new social language (Gee 1999a), one that reflects the differential politics of the time. People position themselves vis-à-vis their own differentiated participation in the social structures they inhabit, that is, airport life, which were affected by September 11. Following the attack, participation in Americanness became categorically differentiated according to ethnicity, religion, nationality, and discourse. As the critical discourse analyst Norman Fairclough suggests: "People produce representations of the social world, including representations of themselves and their productive activities—people never simply act, their representations of their actions and domains of action are an inherent part of action, action is reflexive. Different representations tend to be produced from different positions" (2000:164).

Again at issue is the question "what are you?" and how people choose to or must position themselves during a catastrophe. Before I could surmise that November day that the neologisms I had heard were particular to the Minneapolis airport area, I heard them again a few hours later in Newark. In Minneapolis, there was an announcement at my gate: "All passengers. We will proceed to *wand* you here at the gate. The *wand-er* will pull individual passengers from the line and ask for your permission to be *wanded*."

As one can imagine, my ears perked up. The only place I had ever heard of a wand was in fairy tales where magic was orchestrated by a wand usually held by a good fairy, or in the Harry Potter book series, where Harry learns to do magic with his wand. I immediately realized that the gatekeeper to the plane referred to the handheld metal detector that has been such a new and September 11 reminder in our lives. The *wanderer* referred to the person who randomly chose people in line for a more extensive search of the person. I heard the same language in Newark where the lines were so much longer and where military personnel helped in the *wanding* of people. (Yes, I have just made a gerund out of *wand*.)

To wand is a transitive verb. It is an action verb carried out by one who knows how to wand people, who are, in effect, *wandees*. There is no magic in the act of wanding. The wanderer is not a fairy or magician, but a person who has been trained and trusted to look, judge, and wand within a few seconds. These are usually not military personnel but airline workers who are doing an important civil service for all of us and who became federal workers when they took on their new wanding identities. While this phenomenon was relatively new to us in our public lives, most countries have had such systems of wanding in place for many years, and not just in airports. Unfortunately for us, Americans in general are not very good at it yet because our perceptions, inexperience, and prejudices often make the wanding less random and more particularly focused. In Minneapolis that November 2001, only young and middle-aged men of darker coloring were wanded. This was interesting to me because the majority of the Minneapolis airport workers, the people who clean and sell us food, books, and magazines, are Somali refugees and immigrants whose language is an Arabic dialect. What might be their perceptions of the wandings? In Newark, during the two hours that I stood in line to get through the metal detectors, only young and middle-aged men and Muslim women who were completely covered and wore the *hijab* were wanded.

Our sensitivity to alternative representations of terrorism has been sparked by the horrors of the 1995 Oklahoma City bombing; student shootings among white, middle-class boys in high schools; the anthrax mail scare; and before that, the Unibomber and countless other atrocities. Yet we continued to wand in very specific and, to my mind, problematic ways. As one anonymous colleague aptly pointed out, "Being wanded has different implications depending upon the social location of the wandee. 'Bob from Montana' with a hunting gun is perceived as a lesser threat than 'Mohamed from Newark' with a pair of nail clippers." (The irony of this statement hit home when I thought of my husband, who is from Montana, and I, who was born in Algeria, had our nail clippers confiscated from the toiletries we carried in our carry-on bags during our last trip together.) The neologisms we create are intimately connected to our actions, our perceptions, and our participation in daily life. *Wanding* is by no means part of an apolitical discursive language. Chouliaraki & Fairclough (1999) underscore the notion that social practices, such as labeling or categorizing, are concretized through the positioning of the individual: "the links between particular discourses and social positions, and therefore the ideological effects of discourse, are established and negotiated in the process of articulation within a practice" (150). For example, in October 2001, I had the opportunity to speak with the mail carrier in my neighborhood, who confided that U.S. postal employees worried about delivering mail to "certain" people (Iraqis and Afghans) in nearby neighborhoods, especially in the context of the anthrax mailings. When I asked who these people might be, it became clear that in *wanding* them by looking at their names, their dress, their coloring, their speech, albeit without the body check, the mail carrier had concluded that these midwest residents were potential threats because they are not Euro American. As the mail carrier articulated the process of wanding, it was clear that that his/her ideology of Americanness was firmly grounded in a discourse of us versus them and that I was not wanded in the same way because I did not fit his/her profile of the typical wandees of whom to be wary.

As I think about our communities in the United States, some of which fly the American flag in a new surge of patriotism, I worry about the fears people have, the words they use, the actions they take. Obviously, we have every reason to be fearful and watchful. The tragic crash of the American Airlines flight on November 12, 2001, had many of us at the edge of our seats frantically hoping, ironically and tragically, that it was an accident, an engine failure rather than another attack. Are there ways that, as participant observers of a catastrophe, we can be more critical of our own participation (wanding), especially as we enter into dialogue with others about these issues? This is a key question, one that alerts us to the fine balance we maintain between protecting ourselves from harm and protecting our civil liberties. We put our trust in the hands of public officials, civil servants, our colleagues, our friends, and our families. How fragile that trust becomes with the onslaught of terror, violence, and, sadly, prejudice. Our very words change and as a result our world changes. This was made all the more evident to me by a Mexican American high school student I recently met during my fieldwork, who said, "I feel safe most of the time in school, but people think I'm Arabic instead of Mexican, and my mom doesn't let me go out after school. So you know, it's hard."

The consequences of September 11 are enormous and far reaching. In some ways that day has highlighted social issues we have faced for decades. In other ways, it has created new ways of being in our homes, communities, nation, and the world. Most of us are adapting. I suggest, as Alan Peshkin (1986) did in his study of Christian fundamentalism and other kinds of fundamentalisms, that we remain vigilant of the emergence of extremist ideologies—there is a distinction here between fundamentalism and extremism in that not all fundamentalists are extremists—and actions that harm the civil liberties of people. In the growing global and digital economy that we inhabit, and as people who live in the United States, we must consciously attempt to recognize how we individually and collectively create the conditions for extremisms and extremists who flourish through our foreign policies and our media. If inventing new words helps us capture who we are in a given moment, then let us invent new words, such as *wanding*, but let us also make certain that the actions those words embody are exercised with caution, intellect, moderation, and understanding and that we all learn from our mistakes, look to our history for guidance, and continue to make steady social progress.

"Ah ha" Moments: Going Back to Dearborn

In their manifesto for the first issue of *Ethnography*, editors Willis and Trondman (2000) commented that as ethnographers they are interested in producing "Ah ha" effects, "where evocative expression through data hits the experience, body and emotions of the reader" (12). The work of the ethnographer is to represent ordinary life in all of its social, political, cultural, and linguistic complexities. In effect, ethnography is both a process and a product (Tedlock 2000), and as such the ethnographer must be attuned to change and be able to recognize it when he or she sees it. Willis and Trondman further explain "Ah ha effects" as moments in which "new understandings and possibilities are opened up in the space between experience and discourse, at the same time deconstructing and reshaping the taken for granted in a particular response to the shape of the social order, a response which transcends dichotomies such as the public/private, social/individual. 'Ah ha' effects fuse old experiences with new ones, thus opening readers' minds toward new horizons" (12).

Such an "Ah ha" moment occurred as I began preliminary fieldwork in an Iraqi refugee community hundreds of miles away from Dearborn. On November 25, 2001, CBS aired a *60 Minutes* segment, "Arab Americans," which focused on Dearborn and the Southend. Importantly, this television segment, a public textual and visual document, featured Yemeni Americans from my own research in the community. As I watched this representation of the community, my past experiences with the people there fused with the new media discourse around terrorism, racial profiling, civil liberties, war, discrimination, and fear. It was a startling and important moment because some of the women on the CBS show were Muslims who had never wanted their images to be captured on film and then made public. Yet there they were, *re*-presenting themselves with regard to their Americanness and Islam and becoming part of a very public domain in order to answer the "what are you?" question. The attacks of September 11, coupled with intelligence and media investigations, conflated the normative public and private spaces I had observed and about which I have written. My informants' roles in their community were drastically changed as they simultaneously became cultural and religious representatives of a group under suspicion for terrorism and public apologists of their Americanness and/or lack of it. As one of the *hijabat* told me on one of my return visits to Dearborn, "We don't know who we are anymore."

The "Ah ha" moment was elaborated further as I listened to an interview in the segment in which an Arab American businessman stated that his community had become a "big prison with invisible boundaries . . . a center of hate crimes" (*60 Minutes News Magazine*, November 25, 2002). The media discourse of discrimination was reshaping how this community perceived itself and was perceived by others, and part of the "Ah ha" moment, for me as a participant observer, meant critically understanding, based on prior fieldwork experiences, how Arab Americans in this community could find ways to create a social order that valued their "in-betweenness" as Americans and immigrants. Prior to September 11, southeastern Michigan was described as a haven for the 250,000–300,000 Arabs and Arab Americans residing there, a place for opportunity and upward socioeconomic mobility. In the television segment, it was clear that the community had become a locus for fear, miscommunication, and suspicion. The segment ended with a comment from the Detroit FBI director, who remarked that he believed that Dearborn, Michigan, a metropolitan suburb of Detroit, included residents who were concealing the support of terrorism. Whether this is an accurate depiction of the situation remains to be seen, but it has effected a strong resistance among community members, who argue that being American means having the right to be critical of U.S. international policy and feeling safe in expressing that right.

During a visit to Dearborn in February 2002, I grew more aware of the fragile geopolitical balance maintained by all Americans in the area. This community cannot live through another terrorist attack in the United States and survive with relatively little harm done to its members. Many of the young women who wear the *hijab* noted that in the weeks following September 11, they remained at home, away from the public spaces of non-Arabs because they were often verbally and physically harassed. Many of the men were questioned and at times taken away by local and federal authorities. The descriptions of their experiences plus those of the *60 Minutes* report became all the more tangible when the *hijabat* angrily shared with me an online student university newspaper article entitled "Islam Sucks," published at Wayne State University. The article was copied and shared among Dearborn community members, most of whom were shocked by its contents.

> Some religions suck more than others, though, and one of them is Islam. It's not Muslims that I dislike—I just dislike their faith.
> Fortunately, we have a secular public school system in America that can deprogram the children of Muslim immigrants and help them adopt more productive values.
> Unfortunately, we have countries like Saudi Arabia where children are taught to make friends with Muslims and adopt their traditions. (Fisher 2002)

These excerpts are symbolic of Islamophobia and the kinds of violence incited by the September 11 attacks. Physical and textual violence serve common purposes. They simultaneously destroy, alienate, and reinforce the status quo and offer little room for reconciliation. For example, the previous excerpt illustrates an ideology of negative assimilation of immigrants in our public schools and the eradication of pluralism, openness, and intracultural rapprochement. The we-them nominalizations in the article point to the adoption of an ideology that characterizes some of the worst social practices in our society, from slavery to today's hate crimes to the crimes designated by the United Nations as crimes against humanity. The author's commentary in the Wayne State newspaper is not a critically constructive "Ah ha" moment in our collective histories, because experience has already taught us that words are articulations of ideologies and that extremist views cause physical violence. According to Sunstein (1999), a professor of constitutional law, the social practice of treating large groups of people as dehumanized objects (as does the author of the newspaper excerpt) and writing about them in that way incites violence. Writing about people abstractly by labeling them as "what are you?" rather than attempting to understand *who* we/they are, objectifies us/them as nonhuman beings who have no hopes, fears, and histories of our/their own. Rhetorical abstraction in our texts is a means of violence just as the stories we write about individuals can help reduce textual and political violence.

Why Public Education in These Times?

The three discourses (what is war, security versus civil liberties, and inclusion versus discrimination) that grew out of the September 11 tragedy will not become less important over time because they are rooted in larger social practices in which power, authority, oppression, and violence are closely connected and still characterize the world in which we live. Fairclough (2000) suggests that "we cannot take the role of discourse in social practices for granted, it has to be established through analysis. Any discourse may be more or less important and salient in one practice or set of practices than in another and may change in importance over time" (1). Until we learn and teach to find ways to change how we ask questions, from "what are you?" to "who are you?" we will continue to struggle with the consequences of global catastrophes such as the September 11 attacks. How we participate in daily life and represent ourselves and others in the work we do must reflect sound notions of civility and hospitality. The words we use should reflect a critical understanding of our world, a continuous quest for inclusion, and a healthy respect for differences and disagreements. The contemporary social practice that generated the neologism *wanding* reminds one of Hannah Arendt's wise counsel: "Words can be relied on only if one is sure that their function is to reveal and not to conceal. It is the semblance of rationality, much more than the interests behind it, that provokes rage" (1969/1970:66).

Arendt's counsel is particularly salient to public education and its role in providing a liberating space for youth, such as the *hijabat*, and their families. Preparing Americans and new Americans for life in U.S. society through public schools is key to promoting understanding, civility, learning, and active political engagement. September 11 incited rage and fear among all Americans, but among the *hijabat*, whose lives were still in the making as they and their families struggled to make decisions regarding further education, marriage, and journeys to and back from Yemen, it had a palling effect on their futures.

Upon my return to Dearborn following the September 11 attack, the *hijabat* jokingly asked whether I was a secret agent or whether I was being followed myself. Our collaborative spirit that had previously characterized our research relationship was strained, and we struggled to find some common ground for our continued discussion of their post–high school lives. One of the *hijabat* observed that the Yemeni and Yemeni Americans had grown more conservative since the attack and had withdrawn their children from school and public settings. Still, all of the *hijabat* stressed that education was necessary for them and their children. Saba commented that she still had the same goals, even if she had not had the opportunity to follow a path to them directly: "To be a successful teacher. To be a successful mother. To be a successful wife. To be a successful daughter. That's it. That's all I plan for. To help my family, to help people and that's why I work where I work now [the community center], which services the public at large."

Saba's comments are indicative of a phenomenon that is uniquely American. People can enter and exit educational institutions at any point in their lives. Following the usual trajectory of high school to college to graduate school or the workforce is not necessarily the only legitimate option. Of course, for these young women, marriage to men from Yemen makes upward educational mobility more difficult. Another of the *hijabat* commented in resignation, "I mean I teach him [my husband English] at home. I ask him why he doesn't take night classes and he doesn't want to. He always relies on me to do all of that. I do the financing [in] the house. I do the budgeting in the house. I do the shopping when he doesn't feel like doing it. He likes to enjoy life but he ignores all the other stuff. Like I take care of the bills. I take care of the appointments. I take care of this for the girls [daughters], that for the girls, get this for the girls, that for the girls."

While it is currently difficult for the *hijabat* to continue their education and manage their marriages, nonetheless they are doing it. They are all intimately connected and committed to their religion and to wearing the *hijab*, even more so following September 11. Their biggest challenge, they say, is reconciling their religion and American education, not only for themselves but also for their children. Layla, for instance, said, "But as an adult now, and after reading the Qur'an, I finally understood the purpose of wearing the scarf and I totally respect it. And I would never disrespect myself and disrespect my parents by taking it off because I'm very grateful that I'm part of this religion and that I'm waring this scarf. I'm so happy. And I still plan to be a middle school science teacher, after we come back from this next trip to Yemen."

Living Ethnography in the Past and Present

People often ask me to tell them what happened to the *hijabat* after I left Dearborn. My first response is that they are living their lives. Nadya was the last in the group to graduate in 2001. She married her cousin from Yemen and lives with her parents and sister in a large multifamily home. Her family moved out of the Southend to east Dearborn, where some Yemeni American families have recently migrated. She never liked or did particularly well in school, so attending college is only a possibility. Aisha did not marry her cousin, as she had feared, after graduating from high school. She married a Yemeni American and enrolled in a community college. She continues to be very private about her life and studious in her goals to become a teacher. Amani married after high school and moved to Texas. I have not heard from her since 2000. Layla, like Aisha, avoided marrying a cousin from Yemen. She enrolled in the community college with every intention of transferring to the local state university and becoming a middle school science teacher. Her education was interrupted by several long-term visits to Yemen, where her older brother married a cousin. She e-mailed me that, since September 11, Yemen sometimes seems friendlier and more open to women who wear the *hijab*. She still plans to continue her education.

When I returned to Dearborn in February 2002, I found that no one talked about Nouria. She had disappeared from the community. After a lengthy interview with Mrs. Dunbar, my key informant who was sometimes in contact with Nouria, I discovered that Nouria had tried to run away from her family because she did not want to marry her cousin, wear the *hijab*, or live in the Southend. They then kidnapped her and drove her across Michigan state lines before being apprehended by police and the FBI. Mrs. Dunbar told me that Nouria, at the time of my visit following the attacks of September 11, was under FBI protection, living with a boyfriend, and working in a retail store outside of the Southend. Her family no longer recognized her as a daughter or sister and did not know where she lived, and the community ignored her existence. I did not have the opportunity to speak with her and was afraid to attempt contact with her and inadvertently lead family and/or community members to her.

Saba prevailed in her choice of a marriage partner. After high school she married an Arab American who is not of Yemeni descent. She still works for the community center and hopes to become a certified teacher in a public school bilingual program. She now listens to music and goes to movies and restaurants with her husband and thinks that one can be a good Muslim despite adopting this popular culture lifestyle. She is still deeply religious.

In February 2002, the two *hijabat* who had been the only two college students during my fieldwork informed me that there were now twenty-two young women from the Southend who were enrolled in the community college or at the local university. They reiterated that after September 11 parents became concerned about their daughters being away from home and that the *hijabat* had to struggle against a new conservatism in order to stay in college.

I would like to continue to know and learn from these young women throughout my life. As I observe world events in the Middle East and the United States unfold and grow increasingly more complicated, I realize that our ethnographic past is part of our present. My own sense of self has greatly changed through this research. At the beginning of my fieldwork, I was pleased and taken aback when one of the *hijabat*'s fathers said to me, "You are like a daughter to us. You can visit and stay with us any time." At the time, I remember being grateful for such generosity. Now I understand that such a statement and invitation can never be taken for granted. A humbling, kind, and most generous compliment I received from one of the *hijabat* as I left the field reminds me that ethnography is about personal contact and understanding: "It seems like I have known you all my life." As I think about this statement, I am aware that it pertains to my "being there." Living ethnography means making sense of the geopolitical past and present within the individual and collective lives of the people we study and about whom we care. I hope we never stop caring.

Notes

Chapter 1

1. Pseudonyms are used throughout the book for people and some places to protect anonymity and confidentiality.

2. A notable exception is Alan Peshkin's (1986) work on schools and Christian fundamentalism in one midwestern community.

3. I owe this insight to Susan Florio-Ruane.

4. Kondo (1990) explores the notion of fragmentation of the self in the Japanese family and in a Japanese company. As a Japanese American in Japan, she writes about the collapse of her identity in her collaboration with informants and as both 'other,' someone who is American, and someone who is the same in the sense that she looks like the informants.

5. Phelan, Davidson, and Yu (1993, 1998) coined the phrase "multiple worlds" to denote families, peer groups, and schools. They have written extensively about adolescents and the adaptation strategies they utilize to move from one context to another within those worlds.

6. I owe this insight to Susan Florio-Ruane during a personal telephone conversation on January 23, 2000.

7. Although Bourdieu and Passeron's work has been applied across many contexts, it is important to remember that it is largely based on the educational aims of Republican France and may not apply in many situations in the United States.

8. The *hijabat* were often not allowed to finish high school if they did not maintain their Yemeni cultural and social norms. I address this issue in several subsequent chapters.

Chapter 2

Adapted from Loukia K. Sarroub, "The Sojourner Experience of Yemeni American High School Students," *Harvard Educational Review,* 71:(3) (Fall 2001): 390–415. Copyright © 2001 by the President and Fellows of Harvard College. All rights reserved.

1. Studies conducted in Europe among students of North African origin show similar school success among high school girls (Hassini 1997; Haw 1998; Raissiguier 1994).

2. When two families agree to marry their children, the prospective groom offers a bride price, which can include currency, livestock, and other goods to the prospective bride's family.

3. During *talaq,* the husband declares three times, "I divorce you." Once that is done, according to the *shari'a*, the divorce is final. However, there is a legally

prescribed period, *iddat,* after the divorce, during which neither husband nor wife can marry. During that time the wife cannot reverse the *talaq,* but the husband has the right to return to her (see Molyneux 1998 for a more detailed explanation).

4. See Shamsavary, Saqeb, and Halstead (1993) for a historical analysis of Islamic education and scholarship in the Arab world.

5. For information about Arab Americans and education in the United States, see Sarroub (2000).

6. Foucault (1977) uses the panopticon as a metaphor for the powerlessness people experience in certain institutions and under certain conditions. According to Foucault, the panopticon, a building designed by sociologist Jeremy Bentham, automatizes and disindividualizes power. For example, "in the peripheral ring of the building, one is totally seen, without ever seeing; in the central tower, one sees everything without ever being seen" (202).

7. Two Yemeni American girls in Cobb High School did not wear the *hijab.* Their families did not live in the Southend, and the girls informed me that they were not pressured to wear the scarf by their parents or neighbors.

8. Families with high status included those whose daughters and wives were good students and good Muslims and those who had managed to build a second home in Yemen, thus giving them a higher status there as well.

Chapter 3

1. By classroom, I do not include the physical education classes or music classes. These are exceptions and do not necessarily count as oases. More will be said about this in Chapter 5.

2. The students in the bilingual program, for the most part, attended ESL classes in the various subjects taught by bilingual teachers in Arabic and English. Once the students were assessed to have the required English skills, they were allowed to attend mainstream classes. Some of the Yemeni boys, however, came to the United States very well educated in mathematics and were able to become part of the mainstream math classes with relative ease. Others were allowed into the art classes because art was an elective.

3. I was not able to obtain an accurate number of students who were married or engaged, because both categories are ambiguous unless there are children and because most Yemeni students did not want to divulge such information. However, the school administrators, teachers, and the *hijabat* did tell me that although there was a small married male minority, it was unusual for boys to be married while in high school, whereas the opposite was true for the girls.

Chapter 4

Adapted from Loukia K. Sarroub, " 'In-betweenness': Religion and Conflicting Visions of Literacy," *Reading Research Quarterly* 37:2 (2002c), 130–48. Copyright © 2002 by the International Reading Association. All rights reserved.

1. Sawyer (2002) suggests that the use of "discourse" as an intellectual concept is problematic in its origins and its use in various academic disciplines. I use it here as a broad concept to denote *ways of being* that encompass talk, action, and performance.

2. The five pillars of Islam include *salah* (daily prayers), *saum* (fasting), *hadj*

(pilgrimage to Mecca), *khums* (the one-fifth tax on savings), and *zakah* (the alms tax).

3. Hadith, or "Traditions," are the recorded words, actions, and sanctions of the Prophet Muhammad. Unlike the [*Qur'an*] or the Hadith Qudsi (Divine Hadith), the Hadith are the Prophet Muhammad's own words, which help explain and clarify the [*Qur'an*] and give practical application (1991a; 1991b).

4. The invitation was scanned from the original. Names of people and places have been blacked out to preserve anonymity.

5. Raï music is a "mixture of Western instruments, local Algerian popular longs and rhythms, American disco, songs of Julio Iglesias, Egyptian instrumental interludes, and Moroccan wedding tunes. . . . The lyrics [as Marc Schade-Poulsen argues] reflect the contradiction between the desire of young men to establish love relationships with women and the fact that this implies a questioning authority of their mothers" (Wulff 1995). The girls were not aware that this music is called "Raï" or that it originates in Algeria or among Algerians living in France. Had they known its history and had they understood all the lyrics, which are sung in different dialects than the ones they know, they may not have approved the music.

6. According to Shamsavary, Saqeb, and Halstead (1993). Remnants of these schools are still visible in the Middle East, North Africa, and the United States. For example, the *maktab* or *kuttab* (writing school) focused on reading and writing. The instructor would teach children literacy skills. As the number of these schools grew, they became instrumental in spreading literacy among Muslims in both the East and the West. Eventually, the *maktab* curriculum also included literature, grammar, proper etiquette and manners, calligraphy, swimming, and horsemanship. The *halgha* (circle school) focused on a particular teacher's teachings. The teacher usually sat on a cushion against a wall while students sat around him in a semicircle. The closer the student sat to the teacher, the higher the student's status in learning. Notebooks were usually checked by the teacher, and discussions were characterized by controversial issues and passionate arguments and debates. The palace school, a school for royalty, had a similar curriculum to the *maktab*. However, in addition to a standard curriculum, the palace school focused on preparing its students for higher education, upper-class society, and employment in government and administration. Students were trained in the social sciences and taught how to be effective orators. The *masjid* (mosque school) was the most common and long-lasting form of elementary education in Muslim societies. These schools were most effective in combining worship with learning. During the early period of Islam, there were 3,000 mosque schools in Baghdad, and 1,200 in Alexandria. These schools played a significant role in transmitting knowledge and learning to Muslims. They continue to do so today. The *madrasah* (university of public instruction) provided a more sophisticated curriculum and education than any of the other types of schools. These schools often were dedicated to the promotion of religious and political education, along with general education and specialized training. They attracted the best professors and included vast libraries. Unlike the other schools, the *madrasah* was supported by generous state funding. The last type of Islamic school was the bookshop, which was essentially a literary salon. These institutions were exclusive to the highly educated classes. With the expansion of bookshops across the Islamic world, book dealers and copyists were fundamental in making books available to the general public, students, and centers of learning. From the bookshops, there evolved libraries, which students were free to use. I have also

provided this description of the Islamic schools in an encyclopedia chapter on American Arabs and education (see Sarroub 2000).

Chapter 5

1. Cobb High School, 1992, multicultural report, in Mr. Laramy's [pseud.] files.

2. Cobb High School, 1993, a discussion with Cobb students regarding their perceptions of inter-ethnic relationships in the school, in Mr. Laramy's [pseud.] files.

3. Cobb High School, April 14, 1997, a Muslim holiday memo to principals and assistant principals from the superintendent of the Dearborn School District.

4. Cobb High School, April 16, 1997, a Muslim holiday memo to principals and assistant principals from the superintendent of the Dearborn School District.

5. Cobb High School, December 1997, letter to parent from an assistant principal at Cobb High.

6. Cobb High School, December 8, 1997, memo to superintendent from an assistant principal at Cobb.

7. Cobb High School, January 23, 1998, letter to director of Education and Outreach, American-Arab Anti-Discrimination Committee, Washington, D.C., from superintendent of Dearborn School District.

8. Cobb High School, December 12, 1997, small group of Arabic student concerns expressed at a meeting, in Mrs. Barnabey's [pseud.] files.

9. Cobb High School, January 20, 1998, plan of action (in response to student and parent concerns regarding Cobb High School).

10. Cobb High School, February 4, 1998, cultural diversity action plan memorandum to all Cobb High School faculty from principal.

11. I would argue that this is not a genuine accommodation. It is more an accommodation to the school's inefficiency (not sending home the letters in time) than to the cultural norms of the Yemeni. It was often awkward for the *hijabat* to know exactly what to do for ceremonies when they had not been alerted ahead of time about how they would be received by the principals. In Chapter 3, I discuss why *hijabat* such as Saba would rather not be touched by men, regardless of context, even at a school award ceremony.

12. Some teachers also complained about hearing too much Arabic spoken in the hallways. With the exception of the students in the bilingual program, English was usually spoken in the classroom. Only in special circumstances, as noted in previous chapters, did the students speak in Arabic during class.

13. Very few teachers identified students as White and Arabic in opposition to each other, as Mr. Zanak does here. The Yemeni and American Yemeni are considered to be Caucasian although they did appropriate the opposition of White and Arabic and referred to themselves as Arab or Arabic. Mrs. Barnabey noted a conversation she had with one of her students on this topic: "Sometimes, when they call themselves, they'll say, let's see, they call like the White students, and I say, 'What color are you?' 'Well, I don't know.' I say, 'Well, you are considered Caucasian too. So, I don't know what you're talking about.' 'Well, you know the American.' I say, 'Really? What country were you born in?' 'Well, America, but you know what I mean' " (Interview, February 10, 1998).

14. Cobb High School, November 19, 1996. Friday release for Muslim students memorandum from superintendent to high school principals and assistants.

15. The community-school liaison staff member also did lunchroom duty and kept a watchful eye on the Yemeni boaters, Yemeni American boys, and non-Arab boys. He was also called upon to give advice regarding proper behavior and dress for certain occasions, such as when a car accident occurred and a Yemeni American boy was killed. He sent a memorandum to all the teachers advising them how they and their students should dress for the funeral at the mosque in the Southend.

16. Cobb High School, January 7, 1997, Muslim boys wearing religious "kuffia" memorandum to all Cobb High School faculty from principal.

Chapter 6

1. The mean grade points of the girls and boys are significantly different based on a z test of 4.089 at $\alpha = 0.05$.

2. Arab girls did not differ significantly from non-Arab girls in terms of GPA, $t = 0.77$, $p > 0.05$.

3. The mean grade points of the Arab and non-Arab boys were not significantly different based on a z test of 1.049 at $\alpha = 0.05$ level of significance.

4. Talking about curses in the Southend was difficult. The *hijabat* did not discuss the topic openly with me unless they were under great pressure, as in Saba's case. These curses are part of what is commonly known in the Western world as "folk Islam," which denotes a belief system that includes spirits, such as witches, genies, and the like, in addition to the use of the medicinal properties of certain herbs and plants. Unfortunately, I was not able to get any kind of response from the *hijabat*'s parents regarding the curses.

Chapter 7

Parts of this chapter are adapted from Loukia K. Sarroub, "From Neologisms to Social Practice: An Analysis of the Wanding of America," *Anthropology & Education Quarterly* 33(3):297–307. Copyright © 2002, American Anthropological Association.

1. I thank one of the reviewers of my article that originally appeared in the *AEQ* who suggested that I question how flexible the ideology of Americanness is for those who live in marginalized immigrant communities. Although explicating this idea goes beyond the scope of this chapter, I think that a flexible ideology of Americanness depends, in some ways, on where a community is located geographically. I imagine that marginalized communities in the Detroit, Michigan, metropolitan area, where historically, more that 56 language groups coexisted, might be perceived differently from, say, a new immigrant community in Iowa or Nebraska, where there has historically been very little linguistic or ethnic diversity.

Bibliography

60 Minutes News Magazine. 2001. Arab Americans. CBS, November 25.

Abraham, N. 1978. National and local politics: A study of political conflict in the Yemeni immigrant community of Detroit. Ph.D. diss., University of Michigan, Ann Arbor.

Abraham, N., and A. Shryock, eds. 2000. *Arab Detroit: From margin to mainstream.* Detroit: Wayne State University Press.

Abraham, S., N. Abraham, and B. Aswad. 1983. The Southend: An Arab Muslim working-class community. In *Arabs in the new world: Studies on Arab-American communities,* edited by S. Abraham and N. Abraham, pp. 164–84. Detroit: Wayne State University Center for Urban Studies.

Agar, M. 1994. *Language shock: Understanding the culture of conversation.* New York: William Morrow and Co.

Alvermann, D. E., K. A. Hinchman, D. W. Moore, S. F. Phelps, and D. R. Waff. 1998. *Conceptualizing the literacies in adolescents' lives.* Mahwah, N.J.: Lawrence Erlbaum.

Alwujude, S. 2000. Daughter of America. In *Arab Detroit: From margin to mainstream,* edited by N. Abraham and A. Shryock, pp. 381–90. Detroit: Wayne State University Press.

Ameri, A., and D. Ramey, eds. 2000. *Arab American encyclopedia.* Detroit: UXL/Gale Group.

Anyon, J. 1981. Social class and school knowledge. *Curriculum Inquiry* 11(1):3–42.

Apple, M. W. 1986. *Teachers and texts: A political economy of class and gender relations in education.* New York: Routledge and Kegan Paul.

———. 1993. The politics of official knowledge: Does a national curriculum make sense? *Teachers College Record* 95(2): 222–41.

———. 1993/1997. *Official knowledge: Democratic education in a conservative age.* 2nd ed. New York: Routledge.

Arendt, H. 1969/1970. *On violence.* New York: Harcourt Brace Jovanovich.

Aswad, B., and B. Bilgé, eds. 1996. *Family and gender among American Muslims: Issues facing Middle Eastern immigrants and their descendents.* Philadelphia: Temple University Press.

Barth, F., ed. 1969. *Ethnic groups and boundaries: The social organization of culture difference.* Boston: Little, Brown, and Company.

Barton, D., and M. Hamilton. 1998. *Local literacies: Reading and writing in one community.* London: Routledge.

Bazerman, C. 1994. Systems of genres and the enactment of social intentions. In *Genre and the new rhetoric,* edited by A. Freedman and P. Medway, pp. 68–94. London: Taylor and Francis.

Bernard, Philippe. 2003. In *Le Monde.* 2003. Fourlar a l'école: L'état des lieux avant le rapport Stasi, December 11, pp. 1, 11–12.

Bernstein, B. 1977. Social class, language and socialization. In *Power and ideology in education*, edited by J. Karabel and A. H. Halsey, pp. 473–87. New York: Oxford University Press.

Bhabha, H. K. 1994. *The location of culture*. London: Routledge.

Bogdan, R., and S. Biklen. 1992. *Qualitative research for education: An introduction to theory and methods*. 2nd ed. Boston: Allyn and Bacon.

Bourdieu, P. 1977. Cultural reproduction and social reproduction. In *Power and ideology in education*, edited by J. Karabel and A. H. Halsey, pp. 488–511. New York: Oxford University Press.

———. 1987. The forms of capital. In *Handbook of theory and research for the sociology of education*, edited by J. G. Richardson, pp. 241–58. New York: Greenwood Press.

Bourdieu, P., and J. Passeron. 1997/1990. *Reproduction in education, society, and culture*. London: Sage Publications.

Bowles, S., and H. Gintis. 1976. *Schooling in capitalist America*. New York: Basic Books.

Brown, L., and C. Gilligan. 1992. *Meeting at the crossroads: Women's psychology and girls' development*. Cambridge, Mass.: Harvard University Press.

Carger, C. L. 1996. *Of borders and dreams: A Mexican-American experience of urban education*. New York: Teachers College Press.

Carspecken, P. F. 1996. *Critical ethnography in educational research: A theoretical and practical guide*. London: Routledge.

Cazden, C. B. 1988. *Classroom discourse: The languages of teaching and learning*. Portsmouth, N.H.: Heinemann Educational Books.

Chouliaraki, L. and N. Fairclough. 1999. *Discourse in late modernity: Rethinking critical discourse analysis*. Edinburgh, Scotland: Edinburgh University Press.

Clifford, G. 1989. Man/Woman/Teacher: Gender, family, and career in American educational history. In *American teachers: Histories of a profession at work*, edited by D. Warren, pp. 293–343. New York: Macmillan.

Clifford, J. 1988. *The predicament of culture: Twentieth-century ethnography, literature, and art*. Cambridge, Mass.: Harvard University Press.

Clifford, J., and G. E. Marcus. 1986. *Writing culture: The poetics and politics of ethnography*. Berkeley: University of California Press.

Connel, R. W. 1987. *Gender and power*. Stanford, Calif.: Stanford University Press.

Cummins, J. 1997. Minority status and schooling in Canada. *Anthropology & Education quarterly* 28(3):411–30.

Davies, B., and R. Harré. 1990. Positioning: The discursive production of selves. *Journal for the Theory of Social Behavior* 20(1):43–63.

Degler, C. 1980. *At Odds: Women and the family in America from the Revolution to the present*. New York: Oxford University Press.

di Leonardo, M. 1984. *The varieties of ethnic experience: Kinship, class, and gender among California Italian-Americans*. Ithaca, N.Y.: Cornell University Press.

Duneier, M. 1999. *Sidewalk*. Chicago: University of Chicago Press.

Eisikovits, R. A. 1997. The educational experience and performance of immigrant and minority students in Israel. *Anthropology & Education Quarterly* 28(3):394–410.

El-Or, T. 1994. *Educated and ignorant: Ultraorthodox Jewish women and their world*. Translated by Haim Watzman. Boulder, Colo.: Lynne Rienner.

Eldering, L. 1997. Ethnic minority students in the Netherlands from a cultural-ecological perspective. *Anthropology & Education Quarterly* 28(3):330–50.

Emerson, R. M., R. I. Fretz, and L. L. Shaw. 1995. *Writing ethnographic fieldnotes*. Chicago: University of Chicago Press.

Erickson, F. 1987. Transformation and school success: The politics and culture of educational achievement. *Anthropology & Education Quarterly* 18(4):335–56.

Erickson, F., and J. Shultz. 1992. Students' experiences of the curriculum. In *Handbook of research on curriculum*, edited by P. W. Jackson. New York: Macmillan.

Fairclough, N. 2000. Discourse, social theory and social research. *Journal of Sociolinguistics* 4(2):163–95.

Finders, M. J. 1997. *Just girls: Hidden literacies and life in junior high.* New York: Teachers College Press.

Fisher, Jo. 2002. Islam Sucks. *The South End: The Official Student Newspaper of Wayne State University.* http://www.southend.wayne.edu/days/feb2002/2262002/oped/islam/islam.html (accessed August 23, 2002).

Florio-Ruane, S. 2001. *Teacher education and the cultural imagination: Autobiography, conversation, and narrative.* Mahwah, NJ: Erlbaum.

Freedman, A., and P. Medway. 1994. Locating genre studies: Antecedents and prospects. In *Genre and the new rhetoric*, edited by A. Freedman and P. Medway, pp. 1–20. London: Taylor and Francis.

Friedlander, J. 1988. Introduction. In *Sojourners and settlers: The Yemeni immigrant experience*, edited by J. Friedlander. Salt Lake City: University of Utah Press.

Foucault, M. 1977. *Discipline and punish.* New York: Vintage.

Ganley, Elaine. 2003. Islamic head scarves face ban. *Lincoln Journal Star*, December 12, sec. C, p. 1.

Gee, J. P. 1989. Literacy, discourse, and linguistics: Introduction. *Journal of Education* 171(1):4–25.

———. 1996. *Social linguistics and literacies: Ideology and discourses.* 2nd ed. Philadelphia: Falmer Press, Taylor and Francis.

———. 1999a. *Discourse analysis: Theory and method.* London: Routledge.

———. 1999b. Reading and the new literacy studies: Reframing the National Academy of Sciences report on reading. *Journal of Literacy Research* 31(3):355–74.

Geertz, C. 1973. *The interpretation of cultures.* New York: Basic Books.

———. 1983. *Local knowledge: Further essays in interpretive anthropology.* New York: Basic Books.

Gibson, M. 1988. *Accommodation without assimilation: Sikh immigrants in an American high school.* Ithaca, N.Y.: Cornell University.

———. 1997. Complicating the immigrant/involuntary minority typology. *Anthropology & Education Quarterly* 28(3):431–54.

Gibson, M., and J. Ogbu, eds. 1991. *Minority status and schooling: A comparative study of immigrant and involuntary minorities.* New York: Garland.

Gibson, M. A., and P. K. Bhachu. 1991. The dynamics of education decision making. In *Minority status and schooling: A comparative study of immigrant and involuntary minorities*, edited by M. A. Gibson and J. U. Ogbu, pp. 63–95. New York: Garland.

Gillborn, D. 1997. Ethnicity and educational performance in the United Kingdom: Racism, ethnicity, and variability in achievement. *Anthropology & Education Quarterly* 28(3):375–93.

Gitlin, A., E. Buendia, K. Crosland, and F. Doumbia. 2003. The production of margin and center: Welcoming-unwelcoming of immigrant students. *American Educational Research Journal* 40(1):91–122.

Goffman, E. 1959. *The presentation of the self in everyday life.* New York: Anchor.

———. 1981. *Forms of talk.* Philadelphia: University of Pennsylvania Press.

Gordon, M. 1964. *Assimilation in American life: The role of race, religion, and national origins.* New York: Oxford University Press.

Graff, H. J. 1995. *Conflicting paths: Growing up in America.* Cambridge, Mass.: Harvard University Press.

Greene, M. 1997. Exclusions and awakenings. In *Learning from our lives: Women, research, and autobiography,* edited by A. Neumann and P. Peterson. New York: Teachers College Press.

Grumet, M. 1988. *Bitter milk.* Amherst: University of Massachussetts Press.

Hall, K. 1995. "There's a time to act English and a time to act Indian": The politics of identity among British-Sikh teenagers. In *Children and the politics of culture,* edited by S. Stephens, pp. 243–64. Princeton, N.J.: Princeton University Press.

Hammersley, M., and P. Atkinson. 1995. *Ethnography: Principles in practice.* 2nd ed. London: Routledge.

Hassini, M. 1997. *L'école: Une chance pour les filles de parents Maghrébins.* Edited by L. Priencipe. Vol. 46, *Migrations et changement.* Paris: L'Harmattan.

Haw, K. 1998. *Educating Muslim girls: Shifting discourses.* Philadelphia: Open University Press.

Haw, K., and M. Hanifa. 1998. Schooling for Muslim students in contemporary Britain. In *Educating Muslim girls: Shifting discourses,* edited by K. Haw, pp. 63–84. Philadelphia: Open University Press.

Heath, S. B. 1982. What no bedtime story means: Narrative skills at home and school. *Language and Society* 11:49–76.

———. 1983. *Ways with words: Language, life, and work in communities and classrooms.* New York: Cambridge University Press.

Hoffman, N., ed. 1981. *Woman's "true" profession: Voices from the history of teaching.* Old Westbury, N.Y.: Feminist Press.

Ibrahim, Ezzedin, and Denys Johnson-Davies, trans. 1991a. *An-Anwawi's forty Hadith.* Beirut, Lebanon: Holy Koran Publishing House.

———. trans. 1991b. *Forty Hadith Qudsi.* Beirut, Lebanon: Holy Koran Publishing House.

Jackson, P. W. 1968/1990. *Life in classrooms.* New York: Teachers College Press.

Kondo, D. K. 1990. *Crafting selves: Power, gender, and discourses of identity in a Japanese workplace.* Chicago: University of Chicago Press.

Kulwicki, A. 1987. *An ethnographic study of illness perceptions and practices of Yemeni-Americans.* Dearborn, Mich.: Arab Community Center for Economic and Social Services.

Labaree, D. F. 1997. Public goods, private goods: The American struggle over educational goals. *American Educational Research Journal* 34(1):39–81.

Lareau, A. 2000. *Home advantage: Social class and parental intervention in elementary education.* New York: Rowman and Littlefield Publishers, Inc.

Lewis, P. 1994. *Islamic Britain: Religion, politics, and identity among British Muslims.* London: I. B. Tauris.

Metcalf, B. D. 1996. Introduction: Sacred words, sanctioned practice, new communities. In *Making a Muslim space in North America and Europe,* edited by B. D. Metcalf, pp. 1–27. Berkeley: University of California Press.

Miles, M., and A. Huberman. 1994. *Qualitative data analysis.* 2nd ed. New York: Sage Publications.

Moje, E. B. 2000. "To be part of the story": The literacy practices of Gangsta adolescents. *Teachers College Record* 102(3):651–90.

Moll, L. C. 1992. Bilingual classroom studies and community analysis: Some recent trends. *Educational Researcher* 21(2):20–24.

Moll, L. C., C. Amanti, N. Neff, and N. Gonzales. 1992. Funds of knowledge for teaching: Using a qualitative approach to connect homes to schools. *Theory into Practice* 31 (2):132–41.

Moll, L. C., and N. Gonzalez. 1994. Lessons from research with language-minority children. *Journal of Reading Behavior* 26 (4):439–56.

Molyneux, M. 1998. Women's rights and political conflict in Yemen, 1990–1994. In *Women, ethnicity, and nationalism: The politics of transition*, edited by R. Wilford and R. L. Miller, pp. 133–49. London: Routledge.

Naff, A. 1985. *Becoming American: The early Arab immigrant experience.* Carbondale: Southern Illinois University Press.

———. 1994. The early Arab immigrant experience. In *The development of Arab-American identity*, edited by E. McCarus, pp. 25–35. Ann Arbor: University of Michigan Press.

Ogbu, J. U. 1982a. Cultural discontinuities and schooling. *Anthropology & Education Quarterly* 13 (4):290–307.

———. 1982b. Origins of human competence: A cultural-ecological perspective. In *Annual progress in child psychiatry and child development*, edited by S. Chess and A. Thomas, pp. 113–40. New York: Brunner/Mazel Publishers.

———. 1987. Variability in minority school performance: A problem in search of an explanation. *Anthropology & Education Quarterly* 18 (4):262–75.

———. 1988. Cultural diversity and human development. *New Directions for Child Development* 42:11–28.

———. 1991. Immigrant and involuntary minorities in comparative perspective. In *Minority status and schooling: A comparative study of immigrant and involuntary minorities.* Edited by M. A. Gibson and J. U. Ogbu, pp. 3–33. New York: Garland Press.

———. 1993. Differences in cultural frame of reference. *International Journal of Behavioral Development* 16 (3):483–506.

Perlmann, J., R. Fogel, and S. Thernstrom. 1988. *Ethnic differences: Schooling and social structure among the Irish, Italians, Jews, and blacks in an American city, 1888–1935.* Cambridge: Cambridge University Press.

Peshkin, A. 1986. *God's choice: The total world of a fundamentalist Christian school.* Chicago: University of Chicago Press.

Phelan, P., A. L. Davidson, and H. C. Yu. 1993. Students' multiple worlds: Navigating the borders of family, peer, and school cultures. In *Renegotiating cultural diversity in American schools*, edited by P. Phelan and A. L. Davidson, pp. 52–88. New York: Teachers College Press.

———. 1998. *Adolescents' multiple worlds: Negotiating family, peers, and school.* New York: Teachers College Press.

Portes, A., and R. G. Rumbaut. 1996. *Immigrant America: A portrait.* 2nd ed. Berkeley: University of California Press.

Proweller, A. 1998. *Constructing female identities: Meaning making in an upper middle class youth culture.* Albany: State University of New York.

Raissiguier, C. 1994. *Becoming women, becoming workers: Identity formation in a French vocational school.* New York: State University of New York Press.

Richardson, L. 2000. Writing: A method of inquiry. In *The Handbook of qualitative research*, edited by N. Denzin and Y. Lincoln, pp. 923–48. Thousand Oaks, Calif.: Sage Publications.

Rodriguez, G. 2001. Identify yourself: Who's American? *New York Times*, September 23, D1.

Rosaldo, R. 1993. *Culture and truth: The remaking of social analysis.* Boston: Beacon Press.

Rury, J. L. 1989. Who became teachers? The social characteristics of teachers in American history. In *American teachers: Histories of a profession at work*, edited by D. Warren, pp. 9–48. New York: Macmillan.

Ryan, M. P. 1981. *Cradle of the middle class: The family in Oneida County, New York, 1790–1865.* Cambridge: Cambridge University Press.

Sarroub, L. K. 2000. Education. In *Arab American Encyclopedia*, edited by A. Ameri and D. Ramey, pp. 121–131. Detroit: UXL/Gale Group.

———. 2001. The sojourner experience of Yemeni American high school students: An ethnographic portrait. *Harvard Educational Review* 7(3):390–415.

———. 2002a. Arab American Youth in Perspective. *Society for Research on Adolescence Newsletter.* Spring:3, 6.

———. 2002b. From neologisms to social practice: An analysis of the wanding of America. *Anthropology & Education Quarterly* 33(3):297–307.

———. 2002c. "In-betweenness": Religion and conflicting visions of literacy. *Reading Research Quarterly* 37(2):130–48.

Sasson, J. P. 1992. *Princess*. New York: Avon Books.

Sawyer, R. K. 2002. A discourse on discourse: An archeological history of an intellectual concept. *Cultural Studies* 16(3):433–56.

Scribner, S. 1984. Literacy in three metaphors. *American Journal of Education* 93(1):6–21.

Shamsavary, P., G. Saqeb, and M. Halstead. 1993. Islam: State, religion, and education. In *World religions and educational practice*, edited by W. Tulasiewicz and C. Y. To, pp. 144–86. New York: Cassell.

Shultz, J., S. Florio, and F. Erickson. 1982. Where's the floor? Aspects of the cultural organization of social relationships in communication at home and at school. In *Children in and out of school: Ethnography and education*, edited by A. Gilmore, pp. 88–123. Washington, D.C.: Center for Applied Linguistics.

Siu, P. 1952. The sojourner. *American Journal of Sociology* 58:34–44.

Smith, J. 1995. Semi-structured interviewing and qualitative analysis. In *Rethinking methods in psychology*, edited by J. Smith, R. Harré, and L. Van Langenhove. London: Sage Publications.

Smith, J., R. Harré, and L. Van Langenhove. 1995. *Rethinking methods in psychology*. London: Sage Publications.

Spradley, J. P. 1979. *The ethnographic interview.* New York: Harcourt Brace Jovanovich College Publishers.

Stevens, Cat/Yusuf Islam. n.d. *Cat Stevens: How I came to Islam.* J. D. C. Series on Islam. Jeddah: Jeddah D'awah Center.

Stevenson, D. L., and D. P. Baker. 1991. State control of the curriculum and classroom instruction. *Sociology of Education* 64(1):1–10.

Strauss, A., and J. Corbin. 1990. *Basics of qualitative research: Grounded theory procedures and techniques.* London: Sage Publications.

Street, B. V. 1995. *Social literacies: Critical approaches to literacy in development, ethnography, and education.* London: Longman.

Suarez-Orozco, M. 2001. Globalization, immigration, and education: The research agenda. *Harvard Educational Review* 71(3):345–65.

Sunstein, C. R. 1999. Is violent speech a right? In *An interdisciplinary reader: Violence and its alternatives*, edited by Manfred B. Steger and Nancy S. Lind, pp. 89–92. New York: St. Martin's Press.

Swanson, J. 1988. Migration and rite of passage in a highland Yemeni town. In *Sojourners and settlers: The Yemeni immigrant experience*, edited by J. Friedlander, pp. 49–67. Salt Lake City: University of Utah Press.

Taylor, C. 1996. *Sources of the self: The making of modern identity.* Cambridge, Mass.: Harvard University Press.

Tedlock, B. 2000. Ethnography and ethnographic representation. In *The handbook of qualitative research,* edited by N. Denzin and Y. Lincoln, pp. 455–86. Thousand Oaks, Calif.: Sage Publications.

Thorne, B. 1997. *Gender play: Girls and boys in school.* New Brunswick, N.J.: Rutgers University Press.

Van Zanten, A. 1997. Schooling immigrants in France in the 1990s: Success or failure of the Republican model of integration. *Anthropology & Education Quarterly* 28(3):351–74.

Varisco, D. 1986. On the meaning of chewing: The significance of Qat (Catha Edulis). *International Journal of Middle East Studies* 18(1):1–13.

Willis, P., and M. Trondman. 2000. Manifesto for ethnography. *Ethnography* 1(1):5–16.

Wolcott, H. F. 1994. *Transforming qualitative data: Description, analysis, and interpretation.* London: Sage Publications.

Wolf, M. 1992. *A thrice-told tale: Feminism, postmodernism, and ethnographic responsibility.* Stanford, Calif.: Stanford University Press.

Woods, P., and M. Hammersley, eds. 1993. *Gender and ethnicity in schools.* London: Routledge.

Wulff, H. 1995. Introducing youth culture in its own right: The state of art and new possibilities. In *Youth cultures: A cross-cultural perspective,* edited by V. Amit-Talai and H. Wulff, pp. 1–18. London: Routledge.

Zine, J. 2000. Redefining resistance: Towards an Islamic subculture in schools. *Race, Ethnicity, and Education* 3(3):293–316.

Zogby, J. G. 1990. *Arab Americans today: A demographic profile of Arab Americans.* Washington, D.C.: Arab American Institute.

———. 1995. *Arab American demographics.* Washington, D.C.: Zogby International.

Index

Acknowledgments

The writing of this book was not a solitary activity. Long before there was a manuscript, a group of people greatly influenced my thinking. Michael Silverstein and Karen Landahl taught me to question critically how people make sense of their lives through language and culture. Gerald Graff and Philip Jackson inspired me to make the intellectual leap from theoretical linguistics and cultural anthropology into literacy studies and education. P. David Pearson, David F. Labaree, Susan Florio-Ruane, Lynn Paine, and Anna Neuman provided the mentoring and inspiration to conduct the research for this book. These mentors read multiple drafts of the manuscript, and their individual and collective insight has served only to make it better. I am particularly grateful for P. David Pearson, David F. Labaree, and Susan Florio-Ruane's theoretical and pragmatic wisdom throughout the evolution of the book.

I also benefited greatly from interaction with various people whose support of my research was generous and thoughtful. While I was in Dearborn from 1997 to 1999, I was fortunate to get to know Diane Denaro Frank and Dahan Al-Najjar. I thank them both for their feedback as I negotiated access into the Southend community and as I shared my writing with them. Special thanks go to Karla Bellingar, who assisted me with the transcription of audiotapes and kept me connected to campus life regardless of where my fieldwork and other projects took me. I wish to thank the Arab Community Center for Economic and Social Services. They generously provided invaluable information about the Arab American community in southeastern Michigan and in the United States. My work was made all the easier because of their support.

Drafts of the chapters in this book have been rewritten at a number of institutions where I was in residence for various periods of time. I am particularly grateful to the Spencer Foundation, Michigan State University, the University of Wisconsin–Madison, and the University of Nebraska–Lincoln. Their grant support enabled me to do extensive research in the field, and this book would not have been possible without such support. The University of California–Berkeley provided an especially good place to complete the manuscript during the 2003 spring semester. Among the people who have taught me some important things in relation to this book and who have supported my writing are Michael Apple, Patricia Baquedano-Lopez, David Callejo-Perez, Paul Conway, Anna Demetriades, Patricia Edwards, Charles Elster, Norman Fairclough, James Gee, Margaret Gibson, Mary Louise Gomez, Beth

Graue, Doug Hartman, Carole Hahn, Diana Hess, Karl Hostetler, Joan Hughes, Glynda Hull, Gloria Ladson-Billings, Margaret Macintyre Latta, Tom McGowan, Aleidine Moeller, Jim O'Hanlon, Diane Ohlson, Todd Pernicek, Tom Popkowitz, Marcela Raffaelli, Rebecca Rogers, John Rudolph, Keith Sawyer, Ingrid Seyer-Ochi, Kathy Schultz, Simone Schweber, Tracy Silva, Carol Stack, Michael Suleiman, Dave Wilson, Stanton Wortham, and all my students in various courses who have asked me provocative and thoughtful questions in response to my work. At the University of Pennsylvania Press, I thank Peter Agree, my editor, who first heard about my work before it was ever a manuscript and e-mailed me at least once a year to say that he was still interested in helping me produce a book. He, along with Ellie Goldberg, Erica Ginsburg, and Laura Giuliani, provided the generous assistance any prospective book writer would appreciate.

Heartfelt thanks go to my family—Kader and Georgia Sarroub, Nina Sarroub-Boyd, Chris Boyd, and Juliette Sarroub Boyd—for their lifelong support and encouragement. Our family's experiences as immigrants in the United States have had a profound effect on my research and have given me the fortitude to forge ahead. My husband, James D. Le Sueur, is an inspiration to me. His energy and his dedication to his research have had a tremendous vitalizing impact on my work. As my intellectual companion, he has been patient and impatient, encouraging and critical. I will always appreciate the books he has brought into my life and our conversations around them. Our son, Sef Sarroub Le Sueur, brings tremendous joy and peace to every day, and for that I am thankful.

The people who deserve my deepest gratitude are the *hijabat* and their families, their teachers and administrators, and their school district personnel. I wish I could show my appreciation by recognizing each individual here, but anonymity was promised. The *hijabat* welcomed me into their homes, community, and school lives, and there are not enough ways to express my respect and admiration for them. I learned so much and will always be grateful that my research brought us together. I am also deeply obliged to Cobb High School (pseudonym) for allowing me access to conduct my research and for all the professional courtesy they demonstrated. I have become a better researcher because of them.

Printed in the United States
98450LV00004B/259-264/A